THE SECRET
DIARY OF
JEREMY CORBYN

Also by Lucien Young

Alice in Brexitland
Trump's Christmas Carol

THE SECRET
DIARY OF
JEREMY CORBYN

A PARODY

EBURY
PRESS

3 5 7 9 10 8 6 4 2

Ebury Press, an imprint of Ebury Publishing
20 Vauxhall Bridge Road
London SW1V 2SA

Ebury Press is part of the Penguin Random House Group
of companies whose addresses can be found
at global.penguinrandomhouse.com

Penguin
Random House
UK

Copyright © Lucien Young 2018

Illustrations © Ollie Mann

Lucien Young has asserted his right to be identified as
the author of this work in accordance with the
Copyright, Designs and Patents Act 1988

First published by Ebury Press in 2018

www.penguin.co.uk

A CIP catalogue record for this book is available
from the British Library

ISBN 9781785039942

Typeset in 11.25/17.8 pt Palatino LT Std
by Integra Software Services Pvt. Ltd, Pondicherry

Printed and bound in Great Britain by Clays Ltd, Elcograf S.p.A.

Penguin Random House is committed to a sustainable future for our
business, our readers and our planet. This book
is made from Forest Stewardship Council®
certified paper.

MIX
Paper from
responsible sources
FSC
www.fsc.org   FSC® C018179

Blessed are the meek, for they shall inherit the earth.

Matthew 5:5

If you grow plants and look after your garden, it gives you time to think, it gives you a connection with the natural world and makes you stronger in everything else you do.

Jeremy Corbyn, Channel 4 News,

12 May 2017

Ohhhhh, Je-rem-eeeee Corrr-byn!
Ohhhhh, Je-rem-eeeee Corrr-byn!

Anonymous

A NOTE FROM MR CORBYN

Those who know me are aware that I've never been one to seek out the spotlight. I would much rather be tending my allotment. Alas, becoming Leader of Her Majesty's Opposition is the sort of misfortune that could befall anyone, and now I can't go anywhere without journalists demanding to know what I think about Brexit, which policies I'd pursue if I were prime minister, and all sorts of other things that are none of their business.

As such, I was, at first, far from inclined to let these private diaries be published. However, two factors persuaded me to go against my instinct. Firstly, Ebury Press agreed that all proceeds would be donated to my favourite Colombian donkey sanctuary.* Secondly, I realised that it was an excellent chance to promote some of the passions of my sixty-nine years: cycling, jam-making, vegetable-based cookery, and – last but not least – radical left-wing

---

* Note from the editor: This was never agreed upon.

politics. If the following chapters inspire just one young person to smash the capitalist regime and bring about a socialist utopia, then this will all have been worthwhile.

The Rt Hon. Jeremy Bernard Corbyn, MP
Guevara Lodge, Islington
2018

2015

THE ALLOTMENT

Chapter One

An unexpected promotion, with unexpected consequences. I meet Julian, my new assistant. Some issues settling into the Leader's Office. Mishaps involving jam and the national anthem. I am inspired to take up the poet's quill.

12th September

What a day! At breakfast, Mrs Corbyn and I finally sampled the gooseberry jam I made back in June, which was excellent. Then I cycled along to the garden centre in Harringay, where I treated myself to a top-of-the-range bird feeder designed by Bill Oddie. After lunch, I sat at the kitchen table, sipping a mug of fair trade tea and thrilling at the prospect of all the chaffinches, goldcrests and dunnocks the new feeder will bring to our back garden.

Popped to the corner shop to buy a can of Whiskas for El Gato. Tomorrow I shall visit the allotment and begin to lay down turnips and brassicas.

THE PRESS

In other news, was elected leader of the Labour Party by a landslide. All very gratifying, but I hope these additional duties won't interfere with the planting schedule.

13th September

It seems that the hopes expressed above were misplaced. In fact, as I write this, I can barely keep my eyes open. The nightmare began this morning. I was wearing my red dressing gown, about to take out the biodegradable food waste. No sooner had I stepped outside my front door than I was confronted by a horde of rabid journalists. Half blinded by camera flashes and deafened by cries of 'JEREMY! JEREMY!' I leaped back inside, slamming the door behind me. Such harassment! And on a Sunday, too! I made my horror known to Mrs Corbyn, who said I should be thankful my dressing gown was closed for once.

After some discussion, we decided that the wisest policy was to ignore the crowd outside and carry on with our day as normal. However, just as I'd managed to settle down and get stuck into a sudoku, the doorbell rang. I walked over and put an eye to the peephole: it was a round-faced young man, wearing a lanyard and a bashful expression. I opened the door a crack.

He said: 'Hi? My name's Julian? The party sent me?'

I ushered him inside before any of the tabloid mob could get their feet in the door.

Soon we were all in the sitting room, calming our frazzled nerves with mugs of herbal tea. The young man explained that his name was Julian Forbes, a recent politics graduate, who had volunteered to work as my aide because, he said: 'I, like, totally believe in your message of change and equality and that.'

I asked how he had come by his socialist convictions.

He said: 'I saw a lot of stuff growing up on an estate – my parents' country estate. Then I went to St Paul's, which is where I was, like, exposed to radical theory for the first time? Plus, I really hated my mum and dad, so I thought reading a bunch of Gramsci would annoy them.'

I said: 'I understand completely – I became a militant Marxist on the mean streets of Shropshire. As I see it, it's easy for a genuinely poor person to

JULIAN

call for state-led redistribution of wealth. It takes a certain character to want that when you're upper-middle class. Welcome to the team, Julius!'

He smiled and shook my hand, then reminded me that his name was Julian. I apologised for the mistake, attributing it to all the commotion outside my door. Why, I demanded to know, were these people so obsessed with me? Julian observed that it might be to do with me being the leader of the UK's largest political party. I'm not sure I want that sort of backchat from an assistant, but we'll chalk it up to inexperience.

Some time later, I became aware of an increase in the noise outside. Peeping out from behind the curtain, I saw a familiar figure ploughing through the crowd of journos, slapping away any camera lens that came near him. It was my dear friend and colleague John McDonnell! I could tell he meant business from his scowling face and rushed to answer the door. Once inside, he rounded on me, shouting: 'For heaven's sake, Jeremy, why are you hanging around the house in a bloody kimono? The left has just taken back the Labour Party after twenty years of Blairite bullshit and you're acting like you're Hugh bloody Hefner!'

I asked whether he would care for a biscuit.

He ignored this, saying: 'We need to devise a strategy to win power and transform Britain into a modern socialist state. You're sitting down with me and I'm not leaving until you've chosen your Shadow Cabinet.'

Twelve punishing hours later, we had our team. We would have been a lot quicker, but for the fact that most senior Labour MPs refuse to serve under me. Well, never mind. John shall be my Shadow Chancellor, largely because he is a loyal comrade with impeccable socialist credentials, but also because he'd shout at me if I said no. Andy Burnham will be made Shadow Home Secretary to keep the Blairites happy. Our Shadow Foreign Secretary will be Hilary Benn – alas, Hilary isn't anywhere near as left wing as his heroic dad, and we disagree on most key policy areas, but hopefully that won't become an issue.

After a while, John said: 'Of course, we'll need to find something for Diane.'

Ah, Diane Abbott . . . The very mention of her name set me off on a reverie. How fondly I remember our motorcycle holiday around East Germany back in '79! We would munch sauerkraut all day, then lie together under the stars, discussing agricultural policy until the break of dawn. Mrs Corbyn isn't so keen on her, but that's only to be expected. Ultimately, we decided that Diane shall be Shadow Secretary of State for International Development. I called to give her the good news myself, making sure to mention that I wouldn't let certain things interfere with our professional relationship.

She said: 'What certain things?'

I said: 'You know, our past association.'

After a pause, she said, in a rather bemused voice: 'That was forty years ago, Jeremy …'

I said: 'Yes, it's unbelievable how these things transcend time and space.'

The relevant appointments having been made, John and Julian finally departed, leaving me to lie on the couch, shattered. I knew that leadership would come with some inconvenience, but I never could have anticipated such wholesale destruction of my weekend! And my trials were not yet over: while I was bringing El Gato in for the night, he rewarded me with a vicious scratch on the back of my hand. I suspect our feline comrade has been unsettled by all the journalists outside!

14th September

My first day in the Leader's Office. I wore my favourite crimson tie, my roomiest chinos and a jacket in guinea-pig beige. I cycled to the Houses of Parliament, where I was met by Julian, who had been kind enough to buy me a coffee. Unfortunately, the beans were sourced from one of the twenty-five countries whose produce I'm currently boycotting, so I sent him back for another.

I'd say I'm a pretty humble guy, but, as Labour leader, I did expect a more enthusiastic welcome at the office. Not whoops, cheers and people jumping up on chairs necessarily – still, something bigger than the forced grins and limp handshakes I received. I can understand the muted response of my new staff, though: they've been exposed to a tsunami of lies told about me by the right, centrists and the moderate left. It will be my task to win them over and I have full confidence that I'll do so in record time.

To that end, I instructed everyone to gather round so that I could make a speech. It went something like this: 'Friends, I know that you've all heard a lot of things about me. If you listen to the press, they'll tell you I'm some kind of radical communist.

Well, I say that's counter-revolutionary propaganda from a bourgeois establishment trying to save itself from a glorious new dawn! I think you'll find I'm really not that different from Ed Miliband – though hopefully I'm a bit more electable, ha ha! That said, there will be a few changes. For instance, I don't believe in traditional work hierarchies or a top-down approach to government. I'm not your boss – in fact, I'm here to serve you. So, if anyone's on the lookout for birdwatching tips or a tasty vegan recipe, my door is always open. Cheers!'

Clearly my words were, if anything, too inspiring, as the audience could only respond with stunned silence. I was then approached by our press officer, who suggested I might be wanting to conduct the new leader's customary interview with Andrew Marr. I told him that I wouldn't, as I feared that doing so would *mar* my day. I looked around, expecting a hearty bout of laughter from the rest of the office, but none came. Clearly, I need to raise these comrades' morale.

Had a meeting with my deputy, Tom Watson, an enthusiastic fan of indie music. He wore a Drenge T-shirt under his suit jacket and proudly showed me his multiple wristbands from Latitude and other music festivals. I confessed that the only albums in my possession are a compilation of world music, *The Best of the Red Army Choir* and Billy Bragg's complete discography.

He said: 'Okay, Jeremy, enough of the small talk. The fact of the matter is, you're our leader, and, as I see it, that's just something we have to live with. Unfortunately for you, most of the Parliamentary Labour Party doesn't look at it that way. You're about as popular with MPs as a used Elastoplast in the Commons swimming pool.'

I replied, with not a little dignity, that I was aware that I'd had my ups and downs with the Blairites, but was sure we could all work together.

Tom said: 'You'd better win them over quick, or, by next year, you'll be nothing more than a difficult question in Trivial Pursuit.'

There followed a long pause. Then he said: 'By the way, have you ever heard Alice in Chains' *Jar of Flies* EP? Massively underrated.'

Later, on my way through the lobby, I ran into Sadiq Khan, one of the thirty-five MPs who nominated me for the leadership (which was the minimum required to get on the ballot). Naturally, I thanked him for this vital support.

He replied, in a quiet voice: 'All I wanted to do was widen the debate.'

Still, I said, without his gesture I wouldn't be leader.

'Don't mention it,' he said. 'Seriously, please don't.'

With that he dashed off, looking queasy. I imagine he must have had the notorious mackerel salad in the Commons canteen.

Returned home to find journalists still camped outside the front door. I'm sure all their flash photography is causing my roses to wilt.

Garden update: squirrels persist in looting the bird feeder, thus making a mockery of that device's name. Though this is galling, I am forced to ask myself whether I have the right to pick favourites among the animal kingdom, and decide whether bird or squirrel shall be fed. I stayed up much of the night musing on this point, until Mrs Corbyn elbowed me in the ribs and told me to stop musing out loud.

15th September

Being Leader of the Opposition, I am expected to fulfil a range of ceremonial functions, and so today I attended a service at St Paul's to mark the seventy-fifth anniversary of the Battle of Britain. Now, as a founding member of the Stop the War Coalition, I am, of course, opposed to any display of militarism. However, I'm happy to make an exception for the brave men and women who stood up to fascism in the Second World War. Unfortunately, the squirrel/bird-feeder issue was still very much on my mind and, during the ceremony, I couldn't help drifting off into abstraction. Before I knew it, a band had struck up and everyone was singing 'God Save the Queen'. So lost was I in my thoughts, that I couldn't remember the words to the national anthem! Just plain forgot the lyrics! I had to stand there quietly, twiddling my thumbs. Fingers crossed nobody noticed ...

Later: People did notice. Received an irate phone call from Tom Watson, who tells me Twitter is awash with angry voices calling me a republican dissident and queen-hating terrorist. I swore to him that my silence had been an accident, but Tom wasn't having it.

He said: 'Jeremy, if you don't sort yourself out, Labour's more screwed than the Clash after Joe Strummer sacked Mick Jones!'

It seems absolutely everyone has it in for me ...

16th September

Today was my first Prime Minister's Questions as Labour leader. I have very little time for the gladiatorial showboating that usually characterises the event – all that hooting and hollering from puce-faced public schoolboys – so I've made the decision to only read out questions submitted by the public. According to Julian, our office has received tens of thousands of emails. When pressed, he admitted that many of these had been offensive statements about yours truly, but still, at least people are engaging.

The team were emphatic that I should put a lot of effort into my presentation. As such, I was poring over my briefing papers at breakfast when Mrs Corbyn happened to mention that Mr Batey, our next-door neighbour, had complained about our 'overgrown' rosebushes. This isn't the first time he's done so; I regard his demand that we prune our roses into oblivion as horticultural crypto-fascism. I became quite animated on this point and, in the process of gesticulating, upset a jar of gooseberry jam from the allotment, which went all over my notes. Naturally, I was aggrieved by this waste of good jam, and only became more so when I realised that it had stuck the pages together and consequently much of the document had been rendered illegible. In the absence of a printer or smartphone, I was forced to make the best of a bad situation. I cycled over to Parliament and proceeded to speak from jam-sodden notes, squinting to determine whether Jim from Ponteland was concerned about 'taxes' or 'Texas'. I managed to get through the session reasonably well, despite a few inevitable stops and starts.

Apparently this view was not shared by the people in my office – when I returned from the chamber, they looked absolutely livid.

To make matters worse, the press is being appalling about yesterday's minor oversight. 'CORBYN SPITS ON WAR DEAD'. 'JEZ SEZ F.U. TO VETZ'. 'HANG THIS TREASONOUS TROT BY HIS BEARD'. And that's before we get into the really harsh stuff … Still, what can you expect from centrist rags like the *Guardian*?

For dinner this evening, I whipped up my famous Chickpea Surprise.* As I brought out our plates, Mrs Corbyn volunteered that she wouldn't mind doing a spot of cooking now and then, especially as

---

*The surprise is more chickpeas.

I'm so busy these days. I was touched by her kind offer, but made it clear that I consider my culinary endeavours a vital blow against traditional gender roles. Plus, it's a win-win situation, what with all the delicious vegetarian fare we get to eat! Unfortunately, Mrs Corbyn wasn't feeling too well, so I had to pour most of her meal on the compost heap.

18th September

It's now been two whole weeks since I last had time to visit the allotment. How overrun with weeds it must be! I relayed these concerns to Mrs Corbyn, and finished by saying: 'If I don't tend to my allotment, it will soon become an a-little-ment!'

Mrs Corbyn remained strangely silent. When I asked if she was feeling all right, she replied: 'I'm fine, it's just that your joke felt a bit laboured.'

'I would hope it *was* laboured,' I said, 'given the party I lead!'

This witticism was received no better than the first, and so I went into the garden to replenish the bird feeder.

19th September

The papers are still being awful. The cream of today's headlines was: JEZ-POT – LABOUR'S LEFTIE LOON IS A TOTAL DICK-TATOR. I decided I needed to clear my head. Usually, I like nothing better than to amble around Islington and have a natter with my constituents, writing down their problems in a black notebook. Nowadays I can't do that, what with the constant threat of being ambushed by journalists, desperate to pry into my views on Trident and the EU. In the end, I decided to go for an invigorating bike ride, taking in the sights, sounds and many smells of north London. Everywhere I went, happy people waved and shouted out: 'You go, Jeremy!', 'Good on you, mate!' and a couple of things I'm sure I misheard.

These excursions always instil in me a tremendous sense of tranquillity and perspective. Sure enough, I found myself reflecting on when I volunteered in Jamaica as a young man. I was a carefree, freshly bearded chap back then, and would often try my hand at poetry. In fact, I was so happy with one verse I submitted it to the

New Statesman. Never heard back, sadly. Anyway, upon returning home, I felt inspired to write the following:

AN ODE TO MY BICYCLE
By Jeremy Corbyn

'Four wheels bad, two wheels good'
George Orwell might have written
If he hadn't been so busy
Having a go at the Soviet Union
Via the medium of animals.
As for me, I'll say it loud and proud:
I like
My bike.
It's better far
Than any car
And benefits both my personal health and that of the
    environment.
I hope this verse inspires
The reader to re-inflate their tyres
And with all drivers make a schism
As we peddle forward to socialism.
Cyclists of the world unite!
You have nothing to lose but your chains!

Not a bad effort, after all these years! I read it to Mrs Corbyn over dinner and she was so overwhelmed by the sentiment of the thing she could barely finish her mung bean linguini.

20th September

Another journalistic atrocity: the *Sun* has chosen to lead with a photo of me on my bike, apparently swerving to avoid a small boy, with the headline SHARP LEFT TURN. The photo is clearly doctored – after all, I'm a highly experienced cyclist, so there was never any danger of me hitting that child. And if there was, it was his fault anyway. John McDonnell is very insistent that I can no longer cycle around Islington whenever the mood takes me. Apparently the security people are concerned that, unless I use a ministerial car, they 'cannot guarantee my safety'.

I said: 'No need to worry about safety. I always wear a helmet.'

John shouted: 'For goodness' sake, Jeremy! What if you get run down by a terrorist?'

I replied: 'Better that than to terrorise the earth with carbon emissions!' I thought this was rather witty, but he didn't seem to see the funny side.

Things were relatively quiet at the office today, so I managed to squeeze in an hour or so of manhole cover spotting. Found a gorgeous specimen: Durham Brothers, Bow Road, London – mosaic pattern with concentric circles. Mrs Corbyn doesn't understand my second life as an operculist and would no doubt prefer I spent these hours on something more productive. However, I see no harm in this hobby of mine. Manhole covers never hurt anybody.

Update: Having consulted Google, it seems that injuries resulting from defective manhole covers are, unfortunately, quite common. Still, I'm not giving up the pastime, mortal peril be damned.

21st September

The *Daily Mail* is reporting that David Cameron, while studying at Oxford, 'placed a private part of his anatomy' in a dead pig's mouth. This is just the sort of baseless *ad hominem* attack that poisons our discourse and distracts from important issues.

That said, it is extremely funny.

Chapter Two

I travel to Brighton. Inauspicious beginnings to
the party conference. I write a decent speech and a
great poem. Celebrations get out of hand, resulting
in embarrassment and a difficult journey home.

27th September

Off to Brighton for my first conference as party
leader! It will certainly make a change to be at the
centre of things, rather than just speaking at fascinating fringe events, like 'Solidarity with Traffic
Wardens' and 'The Future of the Cheese Industry'.
Mrs Corbyn has chosen not to come. She says she
would love nothing more, but worries that she would
be a distraction from my leaderly duties. I trust in her
sincerity, though I do note that she's ordered several
bottles of Prosecco on the weekly shop and updated
her Netflix queue with various films I consider to be
barely concealed American propaganda.

Grabbed the 8:15 from Victoria. As a lifelong socialist, I unconditionally love all forms of public transport. That being said, I tend to have unpleasant experiences on trains, and this trip was no exception. For starters, there was no fair trade coffee available from the buffet car. After some discussion, Julian and I concluded that the social change I could achieve by being alert outweighed the evil of buying an unfair coffee. However, the moment I picked up the cup, its plastic lid flew off and the majority of the scalding liquid went down my shirt front. My first instinct was to shout at the server for not attaching the lid more securely, but that would have been a violation of class solidarity. As an under-unionised victim of the private rail industry, he was doubtless exhausted by having to work untenable hours, so I kept quiet and retreated to a toilet to rinse my shirt. While struggling to fit my soiled garment in the tiny sink, I must have activated the hand-drier's motion sensor, which caused the shirt to be blown out of my hands, and the left sleeve to fall in the toilet bowl. In my haste to retrieve it, I inadvertently elbowed the 'Open Door' button, causing my bare torso to be exposed to the rest of the carriage.

I'm sorry to report that my fellow passengers let themselves down by laughing at my misfortune.

If I thought these indignities might abate when I reached the hotel,' then more fool me. As an ardent republican, I had naturally refused the party's offer of a 'king-sized' room, but at the very least I was expecting to have one to myself. Alas, having arrived at reception, I was informed by the spotty young man behind the desk that my suite was double-booked and so I would have to share with Julian. Again, I didn't want to add to the oppression of the proletariat, so kept any resentful feelings to myself as I was handed my key.

Now, I'm not one to indulge in conspiracy theories, but all of my cabinet colleagues seem to have ended up with suites considerably larger and more luxurious than mine. Not that I require luxury – I'm a humble man and so can make do with a humble hotel room. In fact, I prefer it. Looked at this way, the whole business has actually worked out in my favour.

Speaking of senior Labour folk, while I was still in the lobby, my former adversary in the leadership competition, Yvette Cooper, walked straight past me. I choose not to see this as a deliberate snub – people are always telling me I have remarkably unremarkable features.

After lunch, John and Diane popped round to my hotel room, suggesting that we head over to Brighton Pier and play some games at the arcade. Apparently it makes you seem more 'relatable' if the press get a photo of you having a go at air hockey or winning a Minion from the claw machine. I had to remind them that I don't approve of games, which tend to create an unhelpful dichotomy of winners and losers. They went off without me, giving me time to read *Das Kapital* on the pebbly beach.

Got back to the hotel around 9 p.m. As I approached my room, dreading the sight of Julian in his pyjamas, I became aware of the sound of thumping bass and many voices coming from Andy Burnham's suite. I knocked on the door, which was soon answered by the man himself, who had a cocktail in his hand and a lampshade on his head. Revellers were mingling behind him, while the sound system played 'Things Can Only Get Better' at full volume.

Andy winced and said: 'Hello, Jeremy. Anything I can do for you?'

I said: 'Oh no, I just heard you having a party and thought I'd swing by.'

He said: 'Ah, sorry, no party here, mate.'

At this point, Tom Watson popped up and clapped Andy on the shoulder, saying: 'Great party, man. Mind if plug my phone into the dock, play some Modest Mouse?'

Burnham turned back to me and said: 'Yeah, so I'm probably heading to bed now? Laters.'

Before I could respond, he had slammed the door in my face. I must confess this hurt my feelings.

28th September

Terrible night's sleep thanks to Julian's snoring. Donned my sandals for an early-morning stroll by the seaside, to wake myself up. Brighton's lovely, though I don't like to be out of Islington too long (unless it's on a cycling trip around a former Soviet bloc country). Still, this is the sort of place I would like to see replicated throughout Britain: 80 per cent of businesses are antique shops, the pubs sell only vegan snacks, and you're never more than ten feet away from a concert of Ugandan psychedelic funk. Plus, they've got the nation's only Green Party MP, which I think is great (though my colleagues beg me not to say this in public).

Returned to my hotel room, where Julian, John, Diane and I put the finishing touches to my big speech. Diane said: 'Maybe you could try and sound a little less – and don't take this the wrong way – bewildered?'

John said: 'Mmm, yes, and it would be great if we could ease off on the pained expressions. You do sometimes seem like you're being held at gunpoint.'

I replied that I *am* being held at gunpoint, along with all my fellow citizens – the gunpoint of income disparity, the gunpoint of unaffordable housing, the gunpoint of NHS cuts.

Diane said: 'Okay, Jeremy, save the speeches for tomorrow.'

I have decided to read my words from a tele-prompter. Ed Miliband got rid of the practice back in the day, opting to memorise his speeches instead. I won't be doing that – if I go learning speeches off by heart, it might force important things out of my brain.

In the afternoon, I went to speak at a fringe event I do every year, entitled 'Improving Britain's Bollards'. This is usually a lot of fun, and I was heartened to see attendance up massively from last year's audience of five. I gave a rather inspiring speech, whizzing through such subjects as bollard placement, minimum girth regulations and the ever-contentious 'steel vs concrete' debate. I thought I was in for a decent round of applause, if not a standing ovation. However, as soon as I finished, I found myself being peppered with irrelevant questions: 'Jeremy, will you be campaigning for Britain to stay in the EU?', 'Jeremy, what do you say to those who claim you're weak on defence?', 'Jeremy, why do you think members of your own party are saying you're unelectable?' When I made it clear I would only be responding to bollard-related queries, there was a brief pause before they continued with their previous lines of enquiry. With a sick feeling in the pit of my stomach, it dawned on me that these new attendees were not bollard enthusiasts at all, but rather members of the hated mainstream media. I mumbled my apologies to the event's organisers and went for a stroll to soothe my jangled nerves.

I don't mind admitting that I felt pretty dispirited with how the conference had gone so far. Still, walking along the High Street, I spotted a very impressive manhole cover, festooned with rhombuses and a proud knop. When I got back to my hotel room, I felt inspired to jot down the following:

MANHOLE
By Jeremy Corbyn

How might this feeble pen of mine extol
The subtle majesty of thee, manhole?
Cast-iron seal that keeps the sewer's stench
From dear old ladies sat upon a bench.
Though functional, your style must be described:
Divinely patterned, beautifully inscribed
So often has it thrilled my heart to see
On thee 'T. Crapper, 1863'
And, furthermore, it makes my eye grow misty
To think of how you represent our hist'ry.
In ev'ry manhole cover I divine
The glories of municipal design.
I stare at thee that I might ne'er forget
The great accomplishments of Bazalgette!

I think this is easily the best poem I've ever written (at least on the subject of civil engineering). I called up Mrs Corbyn to read it down the phone, and she was suitably impressed.

29th September

After a fitful sleep, I awoke on the day of the big speech. Was I nervous? Yes, I can't deny that. I was more nervous than the time I spilled a bowl of soup on John Prescott. Perhaps I should have spent last night learning my speech instead of writing that manhole poem ... Unfortunately, I had no time to rehearse beforehand, as I'd agreed to speak at the event 'Hummus and Hamas – Building Solidarity Through Middle Eastern Cooking'.

It turns out I needn't have worried – my words were rapturously received. Even though my MPs are determined to act like a bunch of sourpusses, the membership still loves me. The delegates cheered so long and so frequently that my twenty-minute speech ended up taking an hour! Exiting the stage, I found my team looking rather grim, considering the applause still thundering behind me. As is so often the case with members of his generation, Julian was glued to his phone screen. When I admonished him for being a typical millennial, he explained that he was checking the Twitter reaction to my speech.

He said: 'The *Mail*'s calling it "the deranged ramblings of an imbecile".'

I said: 'Could be worse.'

He said: 'This is from the *Sun*: "Like watching your grandad shuffle around the nursing home."'

I said: 'Not terribly constructive. But what do you expect from those right-wing rags? How about the friendly papers?'

He said: 'The guy from the *Mirror* just tweeted that he's had enough, so he's heading down the pub.'

I turned to John and Diane and said: 'Who cares what the commentariat thinks? I've never seen a conference crowd so fired up.'

John said: 'That's all very well, Jeremy, but those are just a few thousand people.'

I said: 'Quality not quantity.'

Diane said: 'I'm pretty sure that's not how elections work …'

At this point, Julian thought it prudent to read out the following: '"An absolute f-ing abomination. The man should be taken out in a field and shot."'

I said: 'Listen, I don't think we need concern ourselves with the words of some anonymous troll.'

He said: 'That was Polly Toynbee.'

Well, the sceptics can cavil and carp all they want. Their voices will be drowned out by the cheering crowds of young people inspired by my message. I'm comfortable that I made an entirely acceptable speech and will now go out to celebrate. In fact, despite my usual abstemiousness, I may even have a drink or two ...

30th September

Horribly hung-over on my way back to London. Last night's merriment got entirely out of hand and I'm afraid I made rather a fool of myself. I arrived at my favourite Brighton pub, the Worker and Comrade, around 7 p.m., where I was greeted with hearty cheers. After leading a spirited rendition of 'The Red Flag', someone handed me half a pint of lager shandy, which I was silly enough to down in one. From that point onwards, I remember only snatches of the evening. I'm ashamed to say I gave the time of Marx and Engels's first meeting as November 1843 instead of November *1842*. Julian tells me that I clattered into our hotel room around 2 a.m., shouting *'VIVA LA REVOLUCION!'*, then kept him up for another hour with a slurred account of Castro's march on Havana.

Was relieved to get home, where I found Mrs Corbyn looking cheerier than she has in yonks. I said, jokingly: 'I hope you haven't been having too much fun without me.'

Dropping a couple of empty Prosecco bottles into the recycling, she smiled and replied: 'No, nothing like that – mainly just ordering takeaways and watching *Sex and the City* ...'

Chapter Three

One Sally Finch is brought in to improve my image. The biased right-wing media step up their attack. I am forced to upgrade my phone. I have a strange and unsettling dream.

1st October

Awful headlines this morning. Some in the office want me to mount a 'charm offensive' with Murdoch et al, but there's really no point. You can't win with these people – just look at Ed Miliband, who got attacked for eating a bacon sandwich the wrong way. In my view there's no right way to eat bacon at all, but that's neither here nor there.

Out of interest, I asked Julian if I could see a full list of the PMQs submitted by the public. After a few attempts to dissuade me, he opened his laptop and showed me the following:

Would the Prime Minister agree that Jeremy Corbyn is a scruffy, clueless throwback who should resign immediately?

This is Dale from Cheadle Hulme. Can the Prime Minister explain why it hurts when I wee?

How come any immigrant can walk into a job as a doctor just cos they have a PhD in medicine?

Oi, Jez, why are you so shit?

Dear Mr Corbyn, I 'poked' my grandkids on Facebook and they have not 'poked' me back. It's been 48 hours – please advise.

Go back to Rusher u hippy!!!1!

jeremy is daddy. i want him to rub that beard all over me lol.

BY REFUSING TO PRAISE COMRADE STALIN, CRYPTO-FASCIST CORBYN HAS EXPOSED HIMSELF AS A NEOLIBERAL TRAITOR. HE WILL BE LIQUIDATED IN THE REVOLUTION.

And so on and so on … and I've left out the really bad ones.

2nd October

Apparently there are those in the party who worry that I'm insufficiently 'cool' to connect with younger voters. What complete rubbish!

Anyway, manhole cover update: Thames Water, hexagonal with pattern of small raised hexagons, by Stanton plc.

5th October

Today I was introduced to Ms Sally Finch, who has been sent over from Labour HQ to 'revamp my image'. I was unaware my image had been vamped in the first place, so this came as something of a surprise. Anyway, a little after lunchtime there was a knock on my office door. I glanced up from my copy of *Ethical Cyclist* to see a stern, business-suited lady in her fifties. She gave me a stiff handshake and shot a disapproving look at the Karl Marx figurine on my desk.

She said: 'I'm a communications and public relations professional, specialising in client-facing solutions and the consumer/trendsetter nexus.

I've been performing image management for senior figures in the party since the start of New Labour.'

I did my best to stifle a wince, then explained to her that we don't like that phrase around here – New Labour is in the past and Old Labour is the future.

She frowned, then said: 'Nevertheless, it's my job to make you seem like a viable prime minister. On that note, I've set up a meeting this afternoon, so that the team can discuss optimising your perception matrix moving forward.'

I just blinked and nodded.

The meeting was more awful than I could have imagined. Sally explained that she wants to make me 'more me', which seems to entail changing every detail of my appearance, behaviour and voice. According to her, it's vital to the party's fortunes that I dress better, as befits a PM-in-waiting.

She said: 'No offence, but you look like a geography teacher whose wife's kicked him out.'

A related goal of Sally's is to stop me wearing my 'Lenin cap'. I pointed out that this headgear wasn't exclusive to Comrade Vladimir, and is also commonly known as the mariner's or fiddler's cap. She responded by questioning this logic, asking if I would wear a Hitler moustache. I told her obviously not – that would mean shaving my beard. Julian attempted to come to my beard's defence.

Sally said: 'I'm sorry, is he here on some kind of work experience?'

Eventually I got bored. These endless meetings make me feel like I'm back in school, which I hated so much that I only got two Es at A Level, in a heroic protest against the oppressive exam board system. Perhaps noting my distraction, Sally raised her voice, saying that I need to show people I can compromise in order to win them over. I replied that the commentariat and the Parliamentary Labour Party may be resistant, but members of the public love me.

She said: 'If only that were the case. We've done extensive polling and these are the results,' then waved a bunch of graphs in front of my face.

I said: 'You can prove anything with numbers.'

She said: 'Fine. We've also been running a series of focus groups with core Labour voters. When asked to choose a word to describe the Leader of the

Opposition, the most common were "catastrophe", "liability" and "shit-pocalypse". With all due respect, Jeremy, you may not like my methods, but you most certainly need them.'

With that, she finally drew the meeting to a close and everyone returned to their desks. I turned to Julian and said: 'Right, that's quite enough for one day. I'm going manholing.'

'Wow, okay …' he replied. 'Is that some kind of Grindr thing?'

After a somewhat awkward exchange, I made it clear that I was referring to my hobby of inspecting manhole covers, rather than having anonymous sex with other men. Not that I have any objection to that sort of thing – I stand in solidarity with our friends in the LGBTQ+ community. The upshot is, I spotted an exquisite coal plate (fleur-de-lis design, John C. Aston & Sons L^D, 70 Essex Road, Islington), so the day did end on a high note.

12th October

Julian seemed glum this morning, so I brought him a cup of tea and asked what the matter was. The lad replied that, while he still believes in our socialist project, the universally negative press coverage has dented his confidence.

I said: 'You can't go getting distracted by what people think. That is, if you even count journalists as people.'

He said: 'But doesn't it, like, get you down, all of them saying you're unfit to be prime minister?'

I replied that I often take comfort in the words of Shakespeare: 'Some are born great, some achieve greatness, and some have greatness thrust upon them.'

He responded: 'Wasn't the character who said that, like, a vain idiot?'

Will have to investigate …

14th October

It's been a draining couple of weeks, so I decided to perk myself up by going on a demonstration. I forget what we were actually marching for or against, but the atmosphere was electric. Young people with piercings and multi-coloured hair kept asking me for 'selfies', and, around lunchtime, I whipped out the Tupperware and started handing out Cajun-style Quorn balls. I had such a splendid day that I didn't realise my mobile phone had run out of battery. Upon arriving home, I plugged it in to charge and was confronted with the following texts:

JULIAN FORBES: Hi Jeremy, was just wondering when you'll be arriving at the office today. Obvs no sweat, J.

JULIAN FORBES: Hi Jeremy, just to let you know that Sally's looking for you. Hit me back when you get the chance.

JULIAN FORBES: Would be super cool if you could call Sally. She's doing a lot of pacing ...

JULIAN FORBES: Okay, so Sally just shouted at me and I gave her your mobile number. Hope you don't mind :(

UNKNOWN NUMBER: Jeremy, this is Sally. Call me back.

UNKNOWN NUMBER: As I'm sure you remember, you're meant to be doing an interview with someone from the Observer. *Please answer your phone, Sally.*

UNKNOWN NUMBER: The guy is sitting in your office and there's only so many cups of tea Julian can make him.

TOM WATSON: Mate, check out Johnny Marr's album Playland *if you get the chance. Obviously it's not up there with the Smiths, but there's definitely a few bangers on there.*

UNKNOWN NUMBER: Jeremy, where on earth are you?

UNKNOWN NUMBER: OH FOR GOD'S SAKE.

UNKNOWN NUMBER: The interviewer has now left. Apparently, in lieu of a profile, he plans to write a piece called 'Jeremy Corbyn – The Invisible Man'.

UNKNOWN NUMBER: In future, I would appreciate it if you could let me know when you're going to pull this sort of stunt.

BATEY (NEXT DOOR): This is your last warning about the roses. If you don't sort them out, I'm cutting them down myself.

Well, there you go – do we need any more evidence that modern technology makes us unhappy?

15th October

In what I suspect is an attempt to keep tabs on me, Sally is insisting I relinquish my trusty old Nokia and start using a smartphone. She says this will help me 'focus on the job at hand'. A device was promptly brought to the office and Julian went about setting it up. I am generally dismissive of such consumerist rubbish, but changed my mind when he started demonstrating the phone's many cool features. The thing's got a built-in camera! Think of all the fascinating manhole covers I'll be able to capture ... Plus, it has the internet, so I can Google facts wherever I am! Spent the rest of the day photographing various drains, then selecting the ideal filter to go with them. So, in a way, Sally *did* keep me focused!

21st October

The press has its knives out once again, this time due to my choice of clothing. In a piece head-lined 'ACCEPTABLE IN THE SEVENTIES', I am accused of being a dowdy 'fashion victim', who exclusively wears outfits that were last in style decades ago. I read out this unprovoked hit piece to Mrs Corbyn at the dinner table. She said: 'To be fair, dear, I've often said your wardrobe could do with an update.'

Perhaps I'm no Georgio Armani, but I think I can rock a canary-yellow short-sleeved shirt as well as the next man ...

26th October

At Sally's behest, we went to Jermyn Street to buy what she called a 'grown-up suit'. While she sat outside the fitting room, tapping away at her iPad, I tried on a selection of outfits. However, the jackets felt too restrictive and the synthetic fabric created static against my skin, so I soon found myself yearning for the sweet embrace of corduroy. I emerged from behind the curtain and explained to Sally that, while I understand she has a job to do, there's no sense in pretending I'm something I'm not. The way I dress is part of the Corbyn deal, like it or lump it. She agreed to resume this discussion another day and took the clothes back to the shop assistant. Unfortunately, the guy kept badgering me, so I ended up buying a tie out of embarrassment. Don't imagine I'll ever wear it – I already own all the neckwear I need (five red ones for work, plus a Wallace and Gromit pattern for light-hearted occasions).

SHOPPING WITH SALLY

29th October

A curious and troubling dream last night. In it, I was woken by the revving of engines and the pungent smell of petrol. Sitting up, I glimpsed, at the foot of my bed, a poodle-haired man with bulldog features, wearing a leather jacket and jeans several times too tight for someone his age.

'Who are you?' I cried, to which he responded, in a growl: 'Only a Loony Left oik would ask that. I'm Jeremy Clarkson, the nation's favourite Jeremy.'

Trying to suppress the quiver in my voice, I observed that he couldn't really be described as such, as the title was surely held by me. The man responded in terms that were ableist regarding my mental health, so I decided to move on, asking him what business he had being in my bedroom.

'I'd say I was the voice of your subconscious,' he replied, 'if that didn't make me sound like an egghead and a poof.'

I attempted to chide this Clarkson for his homophobic language, but doing so sent him into a pink-faced paroxysm about 'liberal snowflakes' and 'political correctness gone mad'. Once he had caught his breath, he proceeded to float through the air, hovering over the bed so that his jowls were inches from my face.

'My point is,' he said, 'how can you hope to lead this country when you have no understanding of the common Brit? Your average bloke won't vote for some sandal-footed, *Guardian*-reading, woman-respecting lentil-lover! No, if you want the man on the street to hear you out, you need to be like me.'

With that he was gone, leaving nothing behind but a whiff of lager and the faint echo of an ethnic slur. I awoke in a cold sweat and was forced to calm myself by listening to the entire A-side of *Now That's What I Call Panpipes!* What on earth could have prompted this hallucination? Perhaps the goats' cheese risotto I had for dinner, which, though delicious, had been in the freezer for several years.

30th October

The headline in today's *Sun*: CHANCELLOR OF THE SEX-CHEQUER: LOONY CORBS WANTS BONKING TAX. I asked around the office and no one has any idea where the story came from. I mean, how would that even work? So much for appeasing the press!

THE NIGHTMARE

Chapter Four

Arrival of The Boy and some alarming news concerning his employment. Joining the Privy Council proves to be a social minefield. My new phone meets an untimely end. Paradise found, then lost, in the form of the Highbury Pottery Club.

1st November

Answered the door this morning and who should be stood there but The Boy! I must confess I was startled to see him – since he moved to Shoreditch, we've heard scarcely a peep. This didn't seem to trouble him, though, as he greeted me with a casual 'Yo Dad, what's up?'

We moved inside, where The Boy – neglecting to take off his shoes – scooped up his stepmother in a vigorous hug. It is a fine testament to Mrs Corbyn that she has always treated The Boy as her own. In fact, she takes his side against me more often than not, which, I must confess, is fairly irritating. While

THE BOY

they exchanged greetings, I took the opportunity to inspect my son. The Boy has always resembled me closely – perhaps a little less rugged and lacking the magnificent beard – but he's looking rather wan these days. I do hope this isn't a sign of dissolution. Then again, I can hardly talk; in my wild youth, I was known to drink most of a pint of cider and talk land reform until the early hours.

As we sat around the kitchen table, each furnished with a hearty bowl of steamed quinoa, The Boy explained the reason for his visit. It seems he has quit his employment at the Kind Hands Organic Seed Company. Of course, I said he should march back to their office and withdraw his resignation immediately, to which he responded: 'It's no good, Dad – they've sacked me! Those guys are so short-sighted and risk-averse – it was all "ethical" this, "sustainable" that. If I'm honest, I'm glad to be shot of the place. That said, there is the question of where I'll be living, now I can't pay my rent …'

After a long pause, I suggested he consider a solid, respectable job, like working on a collective farm.

He said: 'Actually, I was thinking of something in finance? Or retraining as a lawyer? Maybe something more entrepreneurial …'

I need hardly tell you that, upon hearing this, I felt the blood drain from my face. The word 'entrepreneurial' has never been uttered in the Corbyn household and I pray to God (in whom, admittedly, I don't believe) that it never will be again. To be fair to The Boy, he was immediately conscious of his faux pas and returned to the subject of accommodation. Naturally, I told him that he had a place with us for as long as he needed it.

'I'm very grateful for that, Dad,' he said. 'It's pretty embarrassing. But, you see, rent in London is so expensive ...'

I said: 'No need to apologise. The lack of affordable housing is a national disgrace. Someone should do something about it.'

'Isn't that literally your job?' The Boy replied.

Talk about gratitude!

Spent the rest of the day helping The Boy move his possessions from the Shoreditch warehouse space where he's been living. We hired a white van man, who soon recognised me as a senior politician, and so devoted most of the journey to providing me with his views on immigration (he's not a fan). I'm a fervent defender of the working

THE BULLIES

class, but sometimes talking to them is quite coun-
terproductive . . .

2nd November

As may have been apparent from the above entry,
I had certain reservations about The Boy moving
in. It gives me no pleasure to say that my doubts
were swiftly confirmed: he chose to celebrate his
first night back in the family home by going out
drinking with his mates 'from the City'. On top
of that, he was surly and hung-over this morning,
vociferously objecting when I played a Gambian
funk record at full volume (a vital part of my
morning ritual).

6th November

To be a socialist at Westminster is to be
constantly subject to abuse from class enemies.
I was innocently Googling facts about London's
sewage system in the Commons dining room
this lunchtime, when I was assailed by those
toff bullies Boris Johnson and Jacob Rees-
Mogg.

Boris cried: 'I say, Moggers, look at Corbo! The bearded shabbaroon goes about spouting communist piffle-paffle, but he's still happy to use a smartphone. Talk about champagne socialism!'

Rees-Mogg smirked and said: *'Cura te ipsum ...'*

I responded that I do not approve of the term 'champagne socialism'. Firstly, I don't drink champagne. Secondly, why should nice things be the reserve of the 1 per cent? As far as I'm concerned, we should have a National Champagne Service, so that anyone who wants champagne can have it! But again, not me – it gives me a headache.

Johnson and Rees-Mogg walked on, chortling and swapping Latin puns. I hoped that my spirited rebuttal had given the poshos pause for thought, but no – a couple of minutes after I'd returned to browsing Joseph Bazalgette's Wikipedia page, I was struck on the side of the head by a bread roll and, looking up, saw the pair of them giggling into their sleeves. Alas, like Gandhi or Nelson Mandela, I must suffer for my beliefs (though neither of them had to deal with the hurling of baked goods).

7th November

I was putting the last of The Boy's boxes in the attic when I slipped off the ladder and did my back a disservice. Fortunately I was only a couple of rungs up, but it was still a nasty shock. Not that you would have known this from The Boy's reaction, which was to hoot with derision and pronounce my tumble 'classic'.

He said, and I quote: 'Bloody hell, Dad, you made a noise like Tarzan caught his dick in a door!'

Mrs Corbyn was less sympathetic than I might have hoped – she says I shouldn't have been wearing such loose sandals. Well, tight footwear increases one's risk of fungal infection, so who's being safety conscious now?

8th November (Remembrance Sunday)

Laid a wreath at the Cenotaph this morning to honour those who died in the two world wars and all wars since. The solemnity of the occasion was slightly undermined by my back, which is still kicking up a terrible fuss. As such, I was only able to give a subtle bow, though I can't imagine anyone will object.

The Boy was out late last night and only deigned to grace us with his presence around 1 p.m. As he looked rather worse for wear, I asked how he was feeling.

He said: 'Not great – had a lamb kebab that didn't agree with me.'

He realised he was in trouble the moment the words left his mouth. I said, with all the restraint I could muster: 'I take it you're no longer vegetarian?'

The Boy assumed an even sicklier shade of green and, after stammering a while, replied: 'Oh, no, I definitely am in principle, but, y'know, every now and then …'

I said nothing and instead went for a nice warm bath, which always calms me down.

9th November

The Boy was out drinking again last night. Apparently someone called Gavin was celebrating a promotion at his private equity firm, so he and a bunch of the 'City boys' went to a wine bar in Shoreditch. I can't say I approve of my son associating with capitalists – if he wants a bit of rowdy excitement, why doesn't he join me at a meeting of the Islington Local Historians? I hope he isn't falling into a life of decadence. The Boy always did have an addictive personality: I quite sensibly banned all sugar from his diet as a child, until one day he got his hands on a rogue pack of Chewits and caused mayhem at Jorvik Viking Centre. A dark day.

10th November

I'm to join the Privy Council tomorrow and some in my office are worried I might not be up to meeting the Queen. John McD said: 'Now, Jeremy, we don't want another anthem-gate on our hands. I'm as much of a republican as you, but – God knows why – the public loves those inbred weirdos.'

I promised to be entirely courteous and spent the rest of the afternoon in my office, practising small talk on a fifty-pence coin.

11th November

I woke up feeling conflicted about today's meeting with Her Majesty. On the one hand, I'm a fervent republican who rejects outright the notion that anyone is born more important than anyone else. On the other, she seems like a very nice old lady and

I didn't wish to be rude. By the time I'd finished my muesli, my mind was made up to follow the necessary protocol. While I remain unwavering in my anti-monarchist principles, I'm also keen not to kick up a fuss.

At my team's pleading, I agreed to take a car to Buckingham P, rather than cycle. I'd never been inside the place before – all very grand. Ran into David Cameron in the waiting room. He gave one of his Flashman grins and said: 'Well, if it isn't the MP for Leningrad South. Fancy seeing you here … I must admit, I was surprised when I heard you were going to bend the knee. Not gone right wing in your old age, have you?' I reacted to these vicious attacks with quiet dignity. In fact, I wish there had been cameras present, so that everyone could see just how quietly dignified I was.

In the end, my nomination ceremony went quite well, barring one unfortunate incident. I had done some Googling on the way to the palace (mainly to work out what the Privy Council actually *does*) and I discovered that it's considered an unforgivable breach of etiquette for any commoner to turn their back on the monarch. As such, I made sure that I was facing Queen Elizabeth straight on from the moment she entered the room. I managed to maintain almost constant eye contact right up until the point at which I had to kneel before the Queen and kiss her hand.

However, as I backed away, disaster struck: unbeknownst to me, one of our monarch's corgis had snuck up behind me. I tripped over the creature quite spectacularly and, in an effort to break my fall, grabbed hold of a nearby wall hanging, which ripped and came crashing down on top of the hound and me. Crawling out from underneath a sea of fabric, I looked at the Queen in horror. Fortunately, she cackled and guffawed, struggling to catch her breath as she slapped her knee with her sceptre. Cameron, on the other hand, didn't see the funny side. Instead, he turned an asphyxiated shade of puce and screamed: 'Corbyn, you oik! That tapestry was given to Henry VIII by the Marquess of Berkeley!'

I said I could only apologise for my clumsiness.

He said: 'Oh, don't pretend it was an accident – you clearly tore it down as an ideological attack on our beloved monarchy!'

I volunteered that, while it's unlikely I could afford to replace the tapestry, I would be happy to ask my friends at the Harringay Embroiderers to have a go at making a new one. Her Majesty very kindly averred that this would not be necessary, as she had 'always hated the bloody thing'. She then ended the meeting, on the grounds that 'one is fiending for a tall glass of gin'. I was slightly surprised, this being some time before lunch, but who am I to judge?

When I reported these events to my colleagues in the Leader's Office, I expected them to be utterly aghast. Instead, they all looked rather relieved. John McDonell said: 'Thank goodness you only fell over – we thought you were going to start quoting Stalin at her!'

13th November

Finally gave in to Sally's entreaties and agreed to go on *Andrew Marr* this Monday. She thinks it's a perfect chance for me to reintroduce myself to the British public and come across as warm and likeable, rather than a grumpy monk with pants made of nettles.

Bought some undershirts (non-nettle-based) at the local market. Spent the rest of the afternoon playing with my phone.

16th November

Spent the morning dreading my interrogation at the hands (and large ears) of Andrew Marr. As the interview was scheduled for 9:45, I decide to go for a walk to calm my nerves. And then I spotted it: square, with pattern of alternating squares and rectangles, Denbigh, EN 124, B 125, R + B ductile. The jackpot! And that's not all – nearby there lay a nineteenth-century drain grate whose manufacturer was unfamiliar to me. However, when I stooped down to photograph it, catastrophe ensued. The phone, being so damnably light and thin, slipped from my grasp and fell through the slats into the sewer. My horror was compounded when I realised that I hadn't the first idea where the Marr interview was supposed to take place. I considered using a phone booth, but realised I'd neglected to memorise any of my colleagues' numbers. This is what modern technology does to you! There was nothing for it but to head back to the office and face the music.

Shortly after I got there, an ashen-faced Sally stormed up to me, demanding to know where I'd been. I explained, causing her to turn yet greyer. 'You dropped your phone *down a drain*?' she said,

THE DRAIN

with a dangerous quiver in her voice. I pointed out that, in my defence, she bore some responsibility: say what you like about my old phone, it was far too chunky to fit through a grate.

23rd November

Wonderful news! I have been given an honour beyond anything I might reasonably have expected: an invitation to join the Highbury Pottery Club! I've lobbied to be a member of this venerable institution for years and had pretty much given up hope. However while checking my emails this morning, I saw that the name 'Howard Bibb, President' had graced my inbox. He said that, while the club was exclusive, and open to only the most ardent potters, my status as a famed Islingtonite and committed hobbyist had persuaded them to fast-track my application! Our first meeting is this Wednesday and I plan to spend the intervening period boning up on Etruscan vases, PMQs be damned! The Boy made a flippant joke about me being 'addicted to pot', which I disapproved of, both as someone who has never taken drugs and as a man who is deadly serious about earthenware.

25th November

I was unable to concentrate at work today. All I could think about was firing, slipcasting and having a good time in the company of like-minded potters. After an interminable wait, I managed to escape the office and make a dash for Highbury. Soon Mrs Corbyn and I were happily sitting at our potter's wheels, throwing, bulging, fluting and incising to our hearts' content. I met so many fantastic people all of whom I expect will become my dearest friends. The only person I didn't click with was a fellow named Greg, whom I accidentally jostled on my way to the bathroom, causing his clay to collapse. Still, I shall make it up to him! I'm sure I'll have plenty of opportunity over our years of wheel-throwing ecstasy.

26th November

Terrible news! I am no longer a member of the Highbury Pottery Club! My dreams now lie as shattered as a dropped pot. It seems that, after yesterday's meeting, Greg went around pouring poison into every ear he could find. It was determined that

the HPC was an apolitical organisation and therefore the presence of a high-profile politician on the
membership rolls could only serve as a distraction
from its core activities. My voice shaking, I read
out the heartbreaking email to Mrs Corbyn. At this
point, The Boy entered and, noticing my despond-
ency, said: 'Wow, Dad, what's with the *glazed*
expression?' This struck me as a low blow, but I was
too mortified to tell him off.

They say a career in politics prepares you for
any ups and downs that life may throw your
way. Whoever 'they' are, they have clearly never
experienced the pain of being rejected from north
London's premier ceramic group. One moment
you're on top of the world, the next you're banned
from using the communal kiln.

In the evening, I sat in my armchair, process-
ing my grief and watching the rain fall. As I went
to the kitchen to prepare a mug of Horlicks, I
noticed that El Gato had been out in the garden
and tracked a load of muddy paw-prints across
the linoleum. I'm sorry to say that I threw some
heated words in his direction. As someone who
prides himself on remaining calm in the face of
adversity, this shook me.

After the trauma of my expulsion from the HPC, I think I have a better understanding of the young men who snap and become suicide bombers.

27th November

Woke up this morning feeling much more stoic about the whole business. Firstly, the HPC would have taken up time better spent on more important things (maintaining my allotment; generating mulch). Secondly, their mistreatment has made me think rather less of the group. To paraphrase Groucho Marx, I wouldn't want to be in any pottery club that wouldn't have someone like me as a member.

Alas, my mood soured when I came downstairs to find El Gato shredding my briefing notes with all the fervour his little claws could summon. Revenge, no doubt, for yesterday's yelling incident. As a result, I gave a fairly shambolic performance at today's meeting of the Parliamentary Labour Party. John McD was apoplectic, even when given an explanation: 'So, you're literally saying the cat ate your homework?'

Well, of course it sounds ridiculous when you put it like *that* . . .

30th November

Another enervating meeting with Sally about my 'image'. Now she's after the beard! Says it makes me look like 'Santa Claus on hunger strike'. I replied, rather firmly, that I have been awarded 'Parliamentary Beard of the Year' no less than five times and, more to the point, Mrs Corbyn says it's my best feature. Imagine if Samson had cut *his* hair just because a focus group told him to!

Chapter Five

*The situation with The Boy becomes untenable, so
I secure him a new position. My office is plagued
with leaks (figurative, not literal). I confront party
disloyalty before taking a much-needed break.*

1st December

I am becoming increasingly concerned about The
Boy. His room is fetid, and when I went in there
to tell him about a particularly impressive star-
ling I'd seen, he barely reacted. I'm convinced that
his current funk stems from a lack of direction.
A person needs a calling, almost as much as they
need food and shelter. I have a calling in the form of
my allotment and, to a lesser extent, politics. What
is The Boy's vocation, I wonder?

2nd December

My son's room is still a tip. I suggested he tidy it, only for him to reply: 'What's the f-ing point? Everything's a f-ing mess anyway!'

I was about to tell him that, while he's under my roof, he'll abide by my rules, then I remembered that I don't believe in private property, so really it's humanity's roof. Very frustrating. Went to the garden to do some composting, which soon cheered me up.

3rd December

Entering the office, I glimpsed a copy of the *Sun* on the coffee table (I would prefer we didn't fill Murdoch's coffers by ordering the thing, but apparently it's important to know what's being said about me). The headline read COMRADE CORBYN IN CORGI COMMOTION. With a sinking feeling, I opened the paper. Sure enough, they had a full account of my unfortunate stumble at the Privy Council, along with a caricature of me backflipping over the aforementioned dog. I asked John if he thought Cameron had leaked the story, to which he

BREAKFAST

replied that, given the timing, he reckoned it came from within the Leader's Office. He said: 'Jez, some-one in here is leaking like a broken fridge. We need to find them and sack them before the results of your last colonoscopy end up on *Newsnight*.' I told him that a witch hunt wouldn't be necessary – there are other ways to instil discipline.

Without wasting a moment, I called a general meeting to discuss the leaks. As one of the world's most humble men, I pride myself on my placid demeanour. However, it occurred to me that this very persona may have given those in my office the impression that they can do as they please. With that in mind, when everyone was assem-bled, I feigned an incandescent rage, stomping around and shaking my fist. At one point, I even attempted to snap a ruler over my knee, but the thing proved remarkably resilient. Once I was finished, the team filed out in silence, leaving only me and John behind. He said: 'Wow, that was quite a performance.'

I said: 'Sometimes you've got to act tough,' to which he responded: 'I'd say that was "certifiable" rather than "tough", but I suppose either could work.'

4th December

Someone leaked the details of the leaks meeting! Today's *Sun* headline was MEEK JEZ PIQUED, FREAKS RE: LEAKS. This was accompanied by an unflattering photo of me, digitally manipulated so as to be sitting in the turret of a Soviet tank.

John said: 'Unbelievable – the bastards are actually leaking about leaks!'

Julian said: 'Whoa, this is just like *Inception*.'

I demanded to know what he meant. He explained that *Inception* is a Hollywood movie. I made it clear that I don't approve of movies, as their bright colours and loud noises distract from good socialist praxis. John called us a pair of idiots and stormed out.

Given the failure of my disciplinary efforts, I've decided to do some investigating. I've made a list of every prominent member of the Labour Party who might want to bring me down (had to send Julian out to buy more notepads). I also attempted some snooping: hiding around corners of the office, crouching behind the water cooler, etc. While I didn't glean any info about the leaks, I did hear several of my staff do unkind impressions of me, and one of them say: 'I'd call Jeremy a political dinosaur, except the dinosaurs were impressive.'

I suppose that's what I get for eavesdropping ...

5th December

Woke up feeling a bit melancholy, so went for a stroll around Camden. Witnessed something on my way back that I felt obliged to get down in poetic form:

UPON SEEING AN ABANDONED BIKE
By Jeremy Corbyn

Proud two-wheeled steed! What fool
Hurled your frame into the murk
Of Regent's Canal
There to rust
For riderless eternity?
You could have taken someone to
A meeting of the local residents' association,
A Peruvian poetry circle,
A talk on Ukrainian tractor production in the Thirties,
Or other wondrous places.

You could have been mine.
Ashes to ashes,
Rust to rust,
The wheels on this bike
Do not go round.

Quite an emotional poem, that one. I'm not ashamed to say I shed a tear while writing it. Perhaps this is the result of an unsettled mind.

7th December

Sat through another 'media strategy' meeting with Sally. The gist of it was that voters are scared by my so-called 'radical politics' and would feel far more comfortable if they got to know my 'human side'. She said: 'I'm thinking we invite a couple of magazines to take photos in your house. You with your wife, the cat, maybe one of your less nerdy hobbies?'

I replied that I am a politician rather than a pop star, and would on no account have a journalist under my roof. Furthermore, I declared: 'This all sounds like personality politics and I'm not a personality.' Now, I can't be certain, but I'm pretty sure I heard John mutter, under his breath: 'He barely *has* a personality ...'

Things went from bad to worse when I returned home. Walking past The Boy's room, I saw that it was still as messy as a pub that had hosted a Bullingdon Club reunion. Thinking it might shame the lad into action, I decided to give the room a tidy myself. While making his bed, I discovered something appalling hidden under the mattress: a copy of Adam Smith's *The Wealth of Nations*. Waves of nausea washed over me, as I desperately tried to think of an explanation. Could the book have been planted there by subversive elements? But no, there was only one conclusion: my own flesh and blood was reading a right-wing economic text, and I would have to confront him with it.

The Boy arrived home around midnight to find me waiting in the sitting room with the lights off. Switching on a lamp, I held up the book and said: 'I believe this belongs to you ...'

He stammered: 'D-Dad, it's not what it looks like.'

I said: 'Oh yes? Well, you'd better have a good explanation for bringing this capitalist filth into my house!'

Of course, he made the usual excuses – he was looking after it for a friend, he was just using it to conceal his porn mags – though eventually he was man enough to admit the truth.

He said: 'I'm sorry, Dad, but I'm interested in the workings of the free market'.

After a long pause, I said: 'Son, this isn't you. The book, the depression, the getting drunk every night, it's all connected. We can get you help – a psychiatrist or something ...'

At this he became rather irate, saying: 'Look, the reason I've been down lately is that I don't know what to do with my life! Not everyone has a one-track mind like you ... I mean, God, Dad, you haven't changed your opinion on anything since 1962!'

I said: 'That's not true at all – I flirted with Marxist socialism before settling on democratic socialism! Plus, I've been married three times!'

There followed a long argument, not without tears, which culminated in our agreeing that The Boy should be exposed to any ideology he wishes, as long as it's a safe amount and he warns me beforehand.

FURY

10th December

Another load of reactionary bile in today's *Guardian*. The article was full of anonymous quotes from 'senior Labour sources' and 'members of the Shadow Cabinet'. One said: 'Jeremy is an unbelievable catastrophe – it's like Chernobyl and the *Hindenburg* had a baby.' 'I like Jeremy,' said another, 'but he once turned up to a Shadow Cabinet meeting fifty minutes late because he was measuring a marrow.'

First the leaks, now this!

Thought I should do something for The Boy after our spat the other night, so I slid a copy of Eric Hobsbawm's *The Age of Empire* outside his door. The thing about parenthood is that you have to let kids come to the truth their own way.

11th December

Marched into Tom Watson's office to have it out with him about the lack of support from my own MPs. I made what I thought was an impassioned and persuasive speech, though much of it was drowned out by the Mogwai album he was playing.

Nonetheless, I pressed on: 'All I'm asking for is a little loyalty.'

He said: 'To be fair, Jeremy, when we were last in power, you voted against the whip more than any other Labour MP. Four-hundred-and-twenty-eight times, if I recall. It seems a bit rich that you'd expect the PLP to toe the line now.'

I decided to leave him to his mid-Nineties post-rock.

12th December

Another Clarkson dream last night. He came drifting in through my bedroom window, murmuring something about Belgians, then, after a beat, turned to face me. He said: 'Oh Lord, I'm haunting *you* again, am I? Well, how's it been going, you leftie twerp? Not too good, judging by your poll ratings ...'

I explained that this wasn't my fault – after all, how am I meant to lead the party to victory when my colleagues brief against me at every turn?

Clarkson replied: 'Urgh, more leftie liberal whining. Here's a better question: Why do you think you can be prime minister when you're too much of a wet blanket to get your own party in shape? You should be telling those MPs that if they don't keep schtum, you'll back over their balls with a steamroller.'

I started to reply that I believe in a democratic form of leadership, with less emphasis on top-down hierarchies, and—

'Bullshit!' said Clarkson. 'A leader's job is to lead. If some little squit questions you, you've got to nip it in the bud. Back in 2006, Richard Hammond started acting like a big shot. You think that crash was an accident?'

He swooped down at me again and I choked on the smell of gasoline and those little tree-shaped air fresheners. 'Listen Jezza, you've got to build work-place relationships based on loyalty and respect. That's how I'm able to run a functioning set.'

I said: 'Didn't you get sacked from *Top Gear* for punching a producer in the face?'

He said: 'Yeah, well, in my defence, I wanted a steak and I was offered soup instead. You won't understand this, as a vegetarian, but no one comes between a man and his meat.'

I happily conceded that I didn't, in fact, understand.

He said: 'Right, I'd better go sit in a four-wheeled penis replacement and say something demeaning about the French.'

With that, he drifted back towards the window and disappeared. I woke up in sweat-soaked sheets with a parched mouth. I should very much like to have a word with my subconscious about all this.

14th December

I have realised that the solution to The Boy's problems is for him to secure a role at Labour HQ. Given his general listlessness and the rightward drift of his politics, this strikes me as a way of killing two birds with one stone (not that I condone any form of avicide). After a few phone calls, I managed to snag him a job in the Comms Office, which is apparently understaffed – they are having trouble recruiting at the moment, for some reason. I briefly worried that my intervention might be seen as hypocritical, given my fierce opposition to nepotism. However, I reassured myself that The Boy would almost certainly have got the position, even if he weren't my son. Some people mistake his inaction for laziness, but really he's just conserving energy until he can find something to really put his mind to. Fingers crossed that this will solve his malaise ...

When I told him, The Boy wasn't as appreciative as I might have hoped.

He said: 'But, Dad, everyone at your work is so miserable and lifeless – it's like *The Walking Dead* meets *Yes, Minister*.'

16th December

A particularly unpleasant exchange with Little Lord Cameron at PMQs today. He went the colour of a bruised pig as he called me a 'chippy allotment bounder' and 'Putin's boyfriend', all the while accompanied by a 'MMMMMMYYYYYYEEEEEEE-AAAAARRRRGGHHH' from the toads on the Tory benches.

Funnily enough, I ran into him shortly after the session had ended. He had resumed a normal human colour and seemed perfectly calm – a world away from the man who had just been yelling epithets at me.

I said, rather stiffly: 'David, I must say I disapprove of your constant personal abuse. It's not constructive and it gets in the way of building a kinder politics.'

Cameron smiled and said: 'Oh, that? That's all just for show. You oughtn't to take things so seriously, old boy. Learn to chillax – I spend most of my time in Downing Street playing Fruit Ninja on my iPad and everything seems to turn out all right for me.'

This only made me angrier, and so I asked him how he was able to sleep at night, while presiding over the brutal austerity that's destroying the welfare state and tearing our nation apart.

He replied: 'It's like we used to say in the Bullingdon Club – if it ain't broke, why not break it, then let Daddy pay afterwards?'

At least it's nearly the holidays – I'll be glad to get away from this place …

25th December, Christmas Day

I tend to think of Christmas as a bourgeois construct that enshrines materialism as a replacement for genuine human connection, but, still, it's nice to have the family together. Today, as I carved the tofurky, I looked around the table at Mrs Corbyn, The Boy, my other two sons and their spouses, and felt like the luckiest subject of late capitalism alive.

I've been using the Christmas break to catch up on my reading (*The RHS Allotment Handbook & Planner*, *101 Facts about Storm Drains* and *Quotations from Chairman Mao Tse-tung*, which I like to revisit each year). Most recently, I finished George Grossmith's *The Diary of a Nobody*. Its protagonist is a guy called Charles Pooter, who has a rubbish beard and potters around Islington doing trivial things, while annoying those around him with his pomposity. Very amusing, but a bit exaggerated, I thought. After all, who in real life would be so lacking in self-awareness?

31st December, New Year's Eve

Well now, we've made it through another solar cycle! Mrs Corbyn and I threw a party to see in the New Year, with kale blinis and quinoa caviar, as well as board games like Cluedo (highly instructive on how class tension can result in outbreaks of violence) and Risk (I always play as Russia). The turnout was pretty decent, considering the spate of illness that seems to have befallen most of the people in our address book. Several members of the Hornsey Tiddlywinks Society attended, as well as Julian

(I made it clear that attending was one of his duties as my assistant) and The Boy (he did everything he could to get out of it, until I threatened to make him start paying rent).

A few hours into proceedings I delivered some prepared remarks, which I thought were quite good and will share with you here:

Allow me to say how delightful it is to see you all here tonight. You are my friends, my family and, most importantly, my comrades. It is especially sweet to be able to relax together after such a tumultuous few months. This has been a mad year, full of cataclysmic events and shocking developments. The Boy lost a job, which has been painful. I gained a job, which has been excruciating. But, in the end, what defines us, as socialists, is our optimism. Our belief that, by working together, we can make the world a better place. So, as dark and overwhelming as 2015 has often been, it seems to me that the only sensible course of action is to be optimistic. I propose a toast to 2016, the year in which everything will start to make sense!

Right, time for bed ... Dear diary, I shall see you next year. Here's hoping it's a good one!

2016

Chapter Six

Boris Johnson declares for Leave and things get all
Brexit-y. Journalists obsessed with my position
on the EU. Outrageous scenes at PMQs. I am
bullied by some posh boys.

17th February

To my great dismay, I have lost all of my entries from
1st January to 16th February! These were the events
leading up to the calamity: by way of marking the
New Year, I had switched from writing in a 99p WH
Smith notepad to the snazzy number Mrs Corbyn
bought me for Christmas. Its ivory-coloured pages
(70 g/m², acid-free, lined) were a dream to write
on, offering the perfect amount of nib-resistance
for smooth cursive. However, something about my
study had been bothering me and, last Saturday, I
realised what it was: the walls are painted a Conservative blue, putting them at complete odds with my
political beliefs. One trip to Homebase later, I set

about daubing the room red. I was very pleased with the results (though Mrs Corbyn said the shade was too loud and gave her a headache). Unfortunately, the paint took a long time to dry, and the fumes remained pungent some four days later. Sitting down to write yesterday's entry, and finding that an open window didn't do enough to banish the pong, I lit a joss stick (I have a tonne of authentic Seventies Nag Champa in the attic). This helped somewhat, but I must have knocked the holder when I got up to fetch a digestive biscuit from downstairs, causing the lit stick to fall onto the open pages. By the time I returned, the notebook was thoroughly scorched and a month of my records rendered illegible! I've bought a notepad of the same make so as not to upset Mrs C, but the thought of those lost entries rankles. As such, I will now summarise their contents to the best of my ability:

Diplomatic relations with our neighbour, Mr Batey, remain fraught. His current gripe stems from his belief that I and/or Mrs Corbyn habitually put food waste in our black bin bags, thus attracting foxes. I hugely resent the suggestion that I would ever ignore the rules of refuse collection – I happen to take rubbish very seriously.

The Boy – though bright and industrious, deep down – has struggled to settle into his role in the Comms Office. His manager claims that he is unreliable, truculent and constantly watching Netflix at his work station. The Boy claims that his manager is old fashioned, small-minded and dismissive of his revolutionary ideas.

He said: 'It's a nightmare, Dad. I want to modernise – set you up on Snapchat, put some memes out there – but I can't get a look in. The only reason they don't fire me is because you're my father.'

I asked him what a 'meme' is. Some time later, I admitted defeat and said: 'Look, every job has its frustrations. Mine's essentially a living hell 99 per cent of the time. But the answer isn't to give up – it's to get your head down, be humble and trust that you'll be rewarded for your hard work.'

He said: 'How are you being rewarded for your hard work? Isn't your approval rating, like, minus twenty?'

Once again my sound advice is met with derision!

Following on from a New Year's resolution to be more open and honest, Mrs Corbyn has told me that my cooking is not to her taste and that she has felt this way for a while. This was, of course, very difficult to hear, but marriages are all about communication. After a tricky couple of weeks, we agreed that she would supervise my culinary endeavours and enjoy veto powers over any shared meal. I suppose I shall have to wait until she's out of town to perfect my kale strudel.

In UK political news, there was a lot of banging on about Brexit, plus the usual moaning about my leadership. There now: we're up to date!

20th February

Was stirred from a reverie about trains by Mr Batey aggressively jabbing at our doorbell. When I answered the door, he pushed his face so close to mine that I was afraid I'd give him whisker burn. He said: 'Listen here, Jeremy, I've tried to be patient with you, but this time you've gone too far!'

He claims that the smell from my compost heap is drifting out of my garden and onto his property, to the extent that it's upsetting his kids. I maintained that I have been following proper compost technique to the letter and am unaware of any excess scent. After an increasingly terse exchange, Mr Batey called me an 'obstinate old git' and stomped off. Honestly, he's even worse than the Shadow Cabinet!

Later, out of curiosity, I went into the garden and stooped to sniff the heap. Pungent, yes, but pleasingly mulchy. I don't know what the man's on about!

21st February

Boris Johnson has declared for the Leave campaign, sending my hopes for a quiet Sunday up in smoke. After days of theatrical silence, he set out his stall in an article for – where else? – the *Sunday Telegraph*. He writes: 'This is a moment to be brave, to reach out – not to hug the skirts of Nurse in Brussels.' A surprising metaphor, given that 90 per cent of the Tory Party seem to have a psychosexual fixation on nurses and nannies.

Switched on the telly to see him puffing and preening in front of reporters, talking about how the decision had caused him a 'huge amount of heartache'. This is ridiculous – Boris has never had a human feeling in his life. Every single action he takes is designed to bring him closer to Downing Street. He was doubtless born trying to win the vote of the obstetrician. People act as though the man is a harmless P. G. Wodehouse character, but he's more like Bret Easton Ellis. It pains me to think that this dead-eyed clown lives in my beautiful Islington!

Apart from anything else, he's not even that funny. I, on the other hand, was once declared a 'laugh riot' by the head of the Crouch End Philatelist Association. Where's *my* invitation to host *Have I Got News for You*?

22nd February

Perhaps inevitably, the Boris bombshell has stirred the pot (mixed metaphor, but it's been a long day). The wretched denizens of the journalistic underworld are pursuing me with renewed vigour: 'JEREMY, WHAT'S YOUR POSITION ON THE EU?' 'JEREMY, WHY ARE YOU DISTANCING YOURSELF FROM THE REMAIN CAMPAIGN?' 'JEREMY, DO YOU EVEN CARE ABOUT ANY OF THIS?' At one point I had to hide in a Costa Coffee lavatory for a quarter of an hour before they moved on. I'm sorry, but I can't be bothered to share my

Brexit opinions with *you*, dear Diary, let alone some creep who spends their days hacking dead kids' phones and rifling through the binbags outside Danny Dyer's house.

Mrs Corbyn went out with friends this evening, so was left to my own devices in terms of dinner. Ended up having a bowl of brown rice with a handful of white rice for dessert.

24th February

I have become more or less inured to Cameron's vindictive assaults at PMQs, but today's vitriol took the biscuit. He made a totally uncalled-for commentary on my dress sense, telling me to, I quote, 'put on a proper suit, do up your tie and sing the national anthem'. Personally, I don't think you should ever mock someone else's appearance, especially if you yourself resemble a finely glazed ham.

26th February

Yet more bullying! I was walking through the Members' Lobby when a sort of plummy bellow stopped me in my tracks.

PMQs

'Jezza, you frightful oik! What in Beelzebub's name are you wearing today?'

I turned to find Boris Johnson and Jacob Rees-Mogg loitering beside the statue of Disraeli.

'Now, Boris,' I replied, in a tone of some dignity, 'our politics shouldn't be about personal attacks or making fun of people's appearances.'

'Sod politics,' he responded with a shake of his blond head, 'I wouldn't let my stableboy be seen in that outfit!'

'*Vestis virum reddit,*' said Rees-Mogg, snickering.

Well, I wasn't going to be mocked in Latin by a man who dresses like a Victorian undertaker. I drew myself to my full height and declared: 'You may think your tailored suits and Savile Row waistcoats make you better than others. But all across Britain, ordinary people are wearing very different kinds of clothes. The scuffed boots of hard work. The torn T-shirts of class struggle. And the yellowed underwear of quiet resolve. I'd rather stand with them than be garbed in all your finery.' With that, I turned smartly on my heel and departed.

I must admit I was quite pleased with this performance. Only once I was back in my office did I realise that I had been wearing my beige jacket inside out and my fountain pen had leaked in the pocket of my shirt. Of course I was mortified, but I maintain that the moral victory was mine.

1st March

Dreamt last night that I was speaking in the Commons chamber, about to make an excellent point about unilateral nuclear disarmament, when I looked down and realised I was wearing nothing but my socks. Everyone started laughing, then Sally approached and commented that at least this was an improvement on my usual outfits. Must admit I was a bit peevish with Sally today, even though it was only her dream self that insulted me.

12th March

Tensions between the Corbyns and the Bateys have spilled over into open warfare! Was at the kitchen table painting a garden gnome in the colours of the Venezuelan flag when I heard an almighty crash from outside. Stepping into the garden, I saw that my fence lay smashed and splintered on the grass, while Mr Batey stood surveying the wreck, near quivering with anger. He said: 'This is your fault, Corbyn! I told you that you were putting too many hanging baskets on the thing!' I responded that my lobelias had been spaced out at careful intervals, and maybe he should have done more to reinforce the fence on his side. At this point, he began waving an aggressive finger in my face. El Gato, no doubt fearing that some violence was about to befall his master and friend, took this opportunity to leap up on my shoulder and scratch Batey's cheek. With a threat to call the authorities and 'have that creature put down', the man stamped on a piece of fence and went back inside. Despite my staunch commitment to non-violence, I must admit I was rather pleased by this turn of events and so gave El Gato twice his usual helping of Whiskas.

13th March

This morning, at Mrs Corbyn's urging, we went next door and invited Mr Batey to dinner. She believes that the neighbourly bond is a vital one and doesn't want her acquaintance with Mrs Batey ruined by their, I quote, 'idiot husbands'.

'Besides,' she said, 'you have so very few friends as it is ...'

Batey was hesitant to accept, until Mrs Corbyn said: 'The thing is, you two just got off on the wrong foot. Jeremy would be the first to acknowledge that he lives in his own little world.'

I'm not sure I have ever acknowledged this, but it seemed to do the trick. The rest of the day was spent in frantic preparation. In terms of food, Mrs Corbyn pleaded with me to pick something up from Waitrose, but I insisted on cooking myself. Surely, I argued, Mr Batey would appreciate the gesture all the more if I had gone to some personal effort. Accordingly, I made a large batch of my couscous and cannellini bean burgers, a treat we only give ourselves once in a blue moon.

Batey arrived around seven and the dinner seemed to be going splendidly at first. Organic wine was flowing – tap water for me – as we let bygones be bygones and set the world to rights. Mr Batey and I soon agreed that our previous quarrels had been silly and that we could each afford to be more receptive to the other's needs. However, I could not help but notice that our guest had barely touched his plate. When he saw me looking at the neglected burger, he said he wasn't feeling too well and proceeded to pick at it

in a laborious manner. Once he was done, I naturally offered him another.

He said: 'Listen, Jeremy, in the spirit of neigh-
bourliness, I've got to be honest with you – your
food is a little bland for my taste.'

I blinked, uncomprehending. Mrs Corbyn
placed a restraining hand on my shoulder, but it
was too late: the dragon within me had been awak-
ened. I said: 'Well, if we're going to be airing that
sort of thing, I should say that your front door is a
horribly tacky shade of green. It's an affront to the
whole neighbourhood.'

This tit-for-tat quickly escalated, with Batey
declaring: 'You're the worst leader Labour's ever
had. In terms of coolness, you make Ed Miliband
look like Shaft. I genuinely half suspect you might
be a double agent for the Tories.'

Now, as these pages attest, I'm a pretty
thick-skinned guy. However, there is one insult,
one vile and poisonous calumny, that, once spoken,
can never be withdrawn. Call me a boneheaded
blunderer and I shall turn the other cheek. Call
me a fatuous fantasist and I shall laugh and shake
your hand. But call me a Tory, or suggest that I
would have anything to do with that toxic brood,

and watch as I transform into a socialist version of the Hulk. I leapt to my feet and cried: 'Get out of my house! We may live next to each other, but I no longer consider you a neighbour!'

Surprised by my vigour, Batey spluttered, then bolted for the door.

It is a confounding fact of my existence that, while I abhor conflicts of any kind, I constantly seem to be getting embroiled in them. I expected Mrs Corbyn to be furious that I had torpedoed her peacemaking efforts, but she was very comforting, telling me that I'd comported myself with bravery and machismo.

She said: 'No one has the right to call you a bad Labour leader except me.'

After a pause, I asked if this meant that she thought I was a bad leader.

'Of course not, darling,' she murmured, then swiftly went to do the dishes.

18th March

Iain Duncan Smith has resigned as Work and Pensions Secretary. He says the latest cuts to disability benefits are too cruel. What's next, Dracula complaining about excessive neck-biting?

21st March

I know this diary has been somewhat whingey of late, but I really must object to all these comments that I'm offering lukewarm support to the Remain campaign, or even sabotaging it. Today I made a full ten-minute speech in praise of the EU, using the strongest language I could muster. I said the organisation 'doesn't do much harm' and has 'some aspects that are more or less not un-decent'.

I stepped off stage to a smattering of applause and was soon collared by Alan Johnson, the head of Labour In for Britain.

He cried: 'What the hell was that?'

I replied that it had been a full-throated endorsement of his campaign.

He said: 'Jeremy, this country's driving towards the edge of a cliff like a lemming in a petrol tanker. Whether I like it or not, you are leader of the Labour Party. I need you to act like you're more excited about staying in the EU than you are about pulling the lint out your navel.'

With that, he unhanded me and strode off. Since everyone's getting on my case about it, I might as well set down here what I think about the European Union. Do I think it's devoid of flaws? No. Do I think it's advantageous to British companies to be part of the customs union? I do. Do I think that phrasing my opinions as a series of vague questions will get me out of this? Maybe. The point is, the leader of a pro-Remain party has to be pro-Remain, and if he thought a certain supranational organisation had imposed merciless austerity on our Greek comrades, and has a neoliberal economic stance which makes socialist change impossible for its member states, that would be entirely his business, wouldn't it?

4th April

Beyond horrified to discover that Batey next door has gone and sold his story to the papers! While scanning the tabloids in my local newsagent, my eye was caught by the headline INDE-FENCE-ABLE. Next to it was a picture of Mr Batey with his arms folded, standing beside the ruins of our partition. The caption read: 'Jeremy Corbyn may be a terrible neighbour, but I'd hate to see him move to Downing Street.' Worse still, when I opened the rag, it was only to find the words HEAP OF NONSENSE, and an illicitly taken photo of my compost. I immediately called Ofcom to register disgust at this violation of my garden's privacy.

Chapter Seven

The Boy reveals himself to be dating an unsuitable woman. Less than ideal results in the local elections. A series of visits from Stormzy. An unpleasant interaction with a certain leader of UKIP. I am told to focus on the referendum.

23rd April

I notice my diary entries have become sparser of late. It's hard to find the time, what with my duties to constituents and all of this EU nonsense. Nonetheless, I shall attempt to do better.

The allotment is faring well this year, especially given the impediments to my tending it. My rocket, asparagus and artichokes have all come up like a dream. In fact, I have recently begun to sow some more unusual vegetables, such as Hamburg parsley, salsify and scorzonera. In cycling news, I bought a dapper new red helmet. It is made of a polycarbonate blend and EPS foam, boasting 18 honeycomb vents and a detachable visor.

Met Barack Obama today. Nice guy, very large ears.

25th April

The Boy was looking more pleased with himself than usual at breakfast this morning. I was glad to see that his mood had lifted and enquired as to the cause.

He said: 'Well, Dad, I've got some pretty big news. It's regarding my love life ...'

It turns out that he has started seeing a young woman he was set up with by Tristram, one of the 'City boys'. I asked her name and the reply was worse than I could possibly have imagined: Anunciata Basildon-Wyck. As Mrs Corbyn cooed and demanded to see photos, I couldn't help but let my spoonful of bran flakes fall back to the bowl. I gently ventured that this girl sounded rather posh.

The Boy said: 'Oh God, yeah, her parents are totally loaded. I think they used to own, like, half of India. Maybe they still do.'

Conscious of the blood pounding in my ears, I weakly murmured that he was a grown man and free to associate with whomever he pleased.

At this, The Boy looked hurt, saying: 'I thought you'd be happy for me.'

I replied: 'I am, of course. It's just ... I never saw you with a member of the upper class.'

He said: 'Hang on – aren't you always saying that love should know no boundaries?'

I said: 'Absolutely. But, I mean ... Don't you think you might be happier with someone from a good, middle-class background? Or, even better, a member of the proletariat?'

The Boy became incensed at this. He accused me of being callous and insensitive, then stormed out. Perhaps it isn't politically correct to say so, but I'm not sure I approve of the upper and middle classes mixing. We should be able to enjoy our own pursuits, while they amuse themselves with sherry, voting Conservative and fox hunting. It's a case of live and let live (unless you're one of the foxes).

After work, returned home to find The Boy's room vacant. Mrs Corbyn explained that he is staying at 'Anunciata's place in Kensington'. I fear we are growing apart.

26th April

Honestly, if I never hear the word 'Brexit' again, it will be too soon. Sally and Tom Watson confronted me in my office: they feel that my interviews on the subject have tended to come across as evasive and shifty.

Tom said: 'You need to stop obfuscating and give some straight answers. Whatever you might think personally, you're signed up to the Remain campaign, so you need to start acting like it.'

Sally explained that, to this end, they wished to conduct a mock interview, in which I was to defend the EU as wholeheartedly as possible.

She began: 'In the event of a narrow victory for Leave, would you be in favour of a second referendum?'

I said: 'I think the important thing here is that the people's voices are heard. Those voices have been heard and they will be heard. We in politics must be all ears and, if we are hearing impaired, a sign language version should be available. The people need to hear that we are hearing them and we need to be hearing that they hear that they're being heard. And if they speak too quietly or have, say, a regional accent, we should be shouting "Pardon?!" I hope that answers your question.'

Tom said: 'Not at all, but let's try another … Jeremy, you voted for Britain to leave the European Economic Community in the 1975 referendum. Why are you now campaigning for Remain?'

I said: 'Look, things were very different in the Seventies. Just look at trousers. Back then, many young males favoured a flared leg, wherein the trouser became wider from the knee downwards. This style was also referred to as the bell-bottom, and I myself was known to rock a pair from time to time. Would I do so now, in 2016? No, I don't think I would. I favour a straight-legged corduroy these days. Next question.'

Sally said: 'Jeremy, stop. That was incredibly vague.'

I said: 'Apologies – trousers are a kind of fabric sheath, which cover one's legs and undercarriage. I've worn them all my life.'

Tom said: 'Okay, let's try one last question while I still have the will to live. Do you believe that Brexit would be bad for UK businesses? And bear in mind, Jez, if you don't give us a decipherable answer, I'll stick your tie in a fax machine and hit "Send".'

I said: 'Do I believe that Brexit would be bad for UK businesses? Well, that really does depend on what you mean by "bad". And by "believe", "Brexit", "UK" and "businesses".'

At this point, Tom let out a rather uncomradely expletive, then he and Sally left abruptly.

Returned home determined to make amends with The Boy. I found him sulking in his room and offered an apology. I said: 'My behaviour yesterday was completely out of order. I trust you to make your own decisions and hope to meet this Anunciata in the near future.'

He said: 'So you won't go calling her a parasite leeching off the blood of the workers?'

I said: 'Son, I'll do everything I can to stop myself.'

6th May

While I firmly believe in the importance of positive thinking, the results of yesterday's local elections leave a lot to be desired. Still, I've chosen to remain sanguine – after all, there's more to politics than winning votes and exercising power! John and Diane, on the other hand, are livid. The pair of them

THE LOCAL ELECTION RESULTS

marched into my office this morning and let me have it with both barrels.

Diane said: 'We're the ones who have to go on TV and defend you. Do you have any idea how hard it is to keep a straight face when Andrew Neil asks if you're electable?'

John said: 'This is insane. We're running against a cascade of twats who love nothing more than to jack up the price of baby food. They've been in power for six miserable years, their leader is a confirmed pig-defiler and we still can't beat them!'

I said: 'Look, I'm happy to concede that these numbers are somewhat ... less than ideal.'

Diane said: 'Less than ideal? Jeremy, it's the worst result for an opposition party since 1982. You do know that we're supposed to be picking councillors up, not losing them?'

I said: 'I think we should focus on the seats we won, rather than the ones we didn't. It's a case of whether the glass is half full or half empty.'

John said: 'No, Jeremy, it's a case of the glass being full of piss and then someone smashing it in our face!'

Ran into David Davis in the Central Lobby, which is never something you want to do. David is a ludicrously hardcore Eurosceptic. He was also in the territorial version of the SAS, so will start banging on about his military credentials at the drop of a hat (or, I suppose, a beret). Given all this, you can imagine why I was alarmed to see him marching towards me.

He said: 'Corbyn, what time do you have?'

I checked my trusty Casio and replied: 'Nearly two o'clock.'

He frowned. 'Oh, you mean fourteen hundred hours!' He lowered his voice to a conspiratorial whisper: 'Look, Corbyn, are you sure you don't want to join the Leave campaign? We could use a leftie like you as cannon fodder ...'

I said: 'That's very tempting, but no,' and made my excuses to leave.

He said: 'Affirmative – I'm due at a rendezvous point anyway,' then attempted to exit the room by doing a series of tactical rolls.

14th May

Received a surprise visitor today! Around 10:30, Mrs Corbyn and I were getting stuck into some quince jam on toast when the doorbell rang. I answered to find a tall young man wearing an Adidas tracksuit and an expression of great enthusiasm. He explained that his name was Stormzy and that he was keen to meet me, because I, Jeremy, was a badman and a don. Inferring that these things were positive, I said: 'Well, I suppose you should come in.'

Once furnished with toast and quince jam, Stormzy explained that he was a musician, specialising in a genre called 'grime'. Apparently, he is not alone in considering me a badman – many artists in the grime community have 'mad love for Young Jeremy' and approve of my robust socialist program. This is certainly one in the eye for Sally et al, who insist that I'm not 'cool' enough! Stormzy and I proceeded to have a fascinating discussion on income disparity, affordable housing and how he might help with Labour's outreach to the young, urban community. For my part, I suggested that he might release a single to educate the youth about collectivist agricultural policy.

He said: 'Yeah, yeah, maybe ...' and changed the subject rather abruptly. Still, it was a pleasure to discuss political matters with a member of the younger generation. I was rather disappointed when, around midday, he had to leave for lunch with someone called JME.

15th May

Stormzy popped round again today. While he's certainly a fine young man, I'm a solitary person who cherishes their free time on a Sunday. Nonetheless, he was insistent that I listen to what he called a 'grime remix' of 'The Red Flag'. He played me the 'demo beat' off his phone and I smiled politely, despite it being far too loud and chaotic for my taste. He asked if I would be inclined to 'spit a verse' and I demurred (wisely, I think). He then proceeded to quiz me on my policies regarding transport infrastructure, devolution and (shudder) the EU. Discussing politics must be a fun weekend activity when you're a rapster . . .

After a couple of hours, during which he resolutely ignored all hints that I might wish to head to the allotment, etc., Stormzy declared that he needed to go to a music video shoot. However, he said I shouldn't worry, as he would be back for dinner tomorrow(!).

STORMZY

16th May

Arriving at the office, I approached Julian (the youngest person I know) and asked if he had ever heard of a musician called Stormzy. He said: 'You mean Michael Ebenazer Kwadjo Omari Owuo Jr, AKA Wicked Skengman and the Problem? I've loved him since he dropped his first EP, *Dreamers Disease*!'

In the nine months Julian has worked for me, I've never seen him become so animated and I must admit to a certain amount of jealousy. When I mentioned that Stormzy had invited himself to dinner at mine this evening, Julian's eyes near popped out his head. He said: 'Jeremy, please, *please* say I can come! As a public-school-educated white man, I love grime more than anything!'

Well, I didn't have the heart to refuse him.

Stormzy arrived at seven on the dot, keen to continue our political discussions. However, his face fell upon spotting Julian, who was quivering as they shook hands. Julian said: 'Oh my God, Stormzy, mate … I might actually be your biggest fan? I had "Shut Up" as my ringtone for, like, five months.'

The grime artist muttered, 'Thanks,' then shot me a look of betrayal. The rest of the meal consisted of Julian peppering the poor bloke with questions about his lyrics, frequent collaborators and cover art, while Mrs Corbyn and I were unable to get a word in edgeways. After half an hour or so, Stormzy rose, apologising that he had to attend a charity function with Nick Grimshaw. I said: 'You must come round again!'

He replied, in a manner that was far from convincing: 'Yeah, yeah, maybe ...'

17th May

I'm afraid that the longer this idiotic referendum campaign goes on, the darker and more xenophobic it gets. I may not be a huge fan of the EU (or any capitalist organisation, for that matter), but I'm certainly not one of those UKIP weirdos whose mouths start frothing at the sight of a baguette. There are two types of UKIP bloke: the ones who wear burgundy chinos and eat a Sunday roast for every meal, and the ones who are perfectly spherical and have rage-induced heart attacks when they see a black newsreader. Somehow, though, this bunch of cavefish who were too wimpy to join the BNP have managed to turn a vote on membership of a supranational organisation into a chance to stigmatise immigrants. The Leave campaign now habitually refers to 'illegal' immigrants 'flooding' across our 'open borders'. Choose Brexit, they claim, and everything will revert to the Fifties, all privet hedges, village fetes and cricket on the lawn, with nary a brown face to trouble you.

All this nonsense makes me sick. For over thirty years I've had the honour to represent a constituency with a high number of immigrants. My life has been infinitely enriched by working with immigrants, laughing with them, celebrating and commiserating with them. I've even married a couple! Come what may, I will always be proud of my work as an anti-racism campaigner and my arrest for protesting apartheid in South Africa.

This evening I felt compelled to embrace Mrs Corbyn and tell her that I will always defend her right to live, work and love in this country. Unless, as threatened, she throws out my stamp collection, in which case she's getting deported. She wasn't amused by that last part.

18th May

The Boy says he and Anunciata (whose middle names, I've discovered, are Hortensia St Marie McGonegal Claridges, by the way) plan to spend the weekend skiing in Klosters. I have no idea when The Boy learned to ski, but kept my disapproval to myself.

I restated my desire to meet the young lady, saying that I hoped he wasn't keeping her away from us. I asked, half-jokingly: 'Are you embarrassed that your old man's not posh enough?'

He replied: 'Oh, that's not why I'm embarrassed of you!'

20th May

Was walking past St Stephen's Tavern when I saw a familiar and ruddy face: it was Nigel Farage, a cigarette in one hand and a pint of lager in the other. He called out: 'Oi, Corbyn, fancy a round?'

I observed, somewhat stiffly, that it was half nine in the morning.

Farage scoffed and said: 'Ha, that's your whole problem. People look at you and see an abstemious killjoy, whereas I'm a man of the ...' (here he let out a belch) '... people.'

I feared the man would engage me in further conversation, so was relieved when he became distracted by a passing barmaid, whose breasts he commented upon in an ungallant manner. I moved swiftly on, reflecting that the chap reminds me of the nocturnal Clarkson in my recurring dream. Farage really is a different order of magnitude, though: a ghastly, purple, toad-faced anachronism. Strange to think that he's fifteen years younger than me.

When people say I'm too blasé about this referendum, I would point them no further than Farage. Many on the Remain side are beginning to panic, but I refuse to believe that the public could be swayed by that alcoholic chancer. Tom Watson feels differently. Today he told me that I need to get serious about campaigning pronto, or he won't be able to prevent a rebellion among the PLP. Given the way they talk about me at the moment, I'd hate to see what an insurgency would look like ...

Tom said: 'You need to stop with this lukewarm crap. The polls aren't looking good for us.'

I said, rather wittily: 'It seems that we're worried about polls, while the other side are worried about

Poles!' My joke didn't have the intended effect. Instead, Tom looked so ferocious that I swore on my honour that I would step up my defence of the EU.

Later: Mrs Corbyn and I have decided to go on a spur-of-the-moment holiday! Details to follow …

Chapter Eight

Mrs Corbyn and I take a restorative trip. I encounter various language barriers, despite my fluency. Interactions with the very public I was trying to get away from. An epiphany while queuing.

23rd May

As mentioned above, Mrs Corbyn and I are heading off on holiday, partly to celebrate my birthday on the 26th, but mainly to get away from the nastiness of British politics. All the squabbling and ill-will is, quite frankly, doing my head in and I would happily spend a few days in an active war zone if that meant escaping it. In the event, our chosen location is Marbella, where we will be able to enjoy sun, sea and sand, as well as utilising our Spanish (Mrs Corbyn is a native speaker and I'm highly proficient myself). The last few days have been a flurry of preparation: booking flights, changing currency, buying numerous pairs of cream-coloured shorts to sport on the beach. At home, The Boy will keep an eye on El Gato (and vice versa).

In the office this morning, I took Julian to one side and explained my getaway plans. He said: 'Oh wow ... This Thursday? Not, like, *after* the referendum?'

I replied that a refreshing break would allow me to come back to campaigning with a surplus of pro-European vigour.

He said: 'Right, it's just ... I don't think Tom Watson will be happy about that. Or Sally, or John, or Diane, or the papers ... In fact, I think pretty much everyone will be super upset.'

I made it clear to him that, firstly, I am the leader, so what I say goes. And secondly, he was on no account to tell any of those people. I said: 'Just do what you can to clear my diary, then let everyone know once I'm in the air.'

The young man looked rather queasy, so I patted him on the back and gave him a thumbs up.

25th May

Tomorrow's my birthday! And what better way to celebrate than by escaping this rotten country? Of course I don't mean that, but it will certainly be a blessed relief to get away from the rain, the greyness and the constant negativity. To this last end, I've decided to leave my phone at home – I doubt there will be any major developments and, if there are, I'm sure Julian will be able to smooth things over.

26th May, Casa del Socialismo, Marbella, Spain

¡Feliz cumpleaños a Jeremy! As I write this, I am sipping a cool *jugo de naranja* (orange juice) and watching the *puesta de sol* (sunset) while sitting on a *silla* (chair) on our *veranda* (veranda).

Things got off to an inauspicious start when it became apparent that I'd set the alarm clock for 3 a.m. rather than 6 a.m. However, Mrs Corbyn had pretty much forgiven me by the time we arrived at Gatwick. We also managed to get to the airport without any members of the public recognising me. Whenever this happens I feel a mixture of relief and concern for my electoral prospects. Annoyingly, I set off the metal detector at security and was baffled as to why, until I realised it was the paperclip I'd been using in lieu of a missing shirt button.

Had an altercation with the guy at the check-in desk, who claimed my suitcase was too big for carry on. I told him that I had personally measured my case's dimensions and they fell comfortably within the range stated on the airline's website. The man insisted they didn't and said that I would have to pay fifty quid for it to go in the hold. Fifty quid! At that point, I decided to deploy a bit of the old Corbyn charm.

I said: 'Listen, mate, I get where you're coming from. We're both victims of an oppressive airline. I'm the customer who's being exploited and you're just a cog in the machine.'

He said: 'Please don't call me a cog, sir … That'll be a hundred quid.'

I said: 'You just told me it was fifty!'

He said: 'I don't believe I did, sir. Now, do you want to get on the plane, or stay here with me?'

This might have escalated further, had Mrs Corbyn not stepped in and volunteered to pay. I railed against the monopolistic practices of the airlines for our entire flight, which I think may have cost me my complimentary bag of peanuts.

My grumpy mood lifted when I looked out of the window and saw the beauty of Andalusia spread beneath us. We soon landed at Málaga airport, then hopped into a waiting taxi. The driver, a nice chap called Alejandro, said: 'English, eh? You guys are going crazy with the Brexit stuff, no?'

I said: 'Nothing to do with me, mate – I'm not into politics.' Once we'd arrived at our villa and unpacked, Mrs Corbyn gave me my birthday present: a brand new Casio wristwatch with built-in calculator! I was touched by this and wrapped her in a warm embrace. Let's just say I'm hoping for another present later tonight …

(Batteries to go with it.)

27th May

Woke to the sound of seagulls and the blissful realisation that I wouldn't have to deal with any MPs or journalists today. Mrs Corbyn was keen to have a lie-in, so I went for a solo wander down the beach. God, it feels good to wear sandals in a country whose weather justifies them!

While observing the flight of a particularly large gull, I stumbled over a pair of sunbathers. They were a couple roughly my age: the man round and sunburned, the woman leathery and wearing a truly enormous hat. The former cried out: 'Oi, watch yourself, mate!'

This, combined with their Union Jack beach towel and the three lions tattooed on the bloke's bicep, led me to conclude that the pair were English. I apologised and we soon got to talking – they introduced themselves as Glenn and Deborah, a married couple from Chelmsford.

He said: 'Don't I know you from somewhere? D'you host a gardening show or something?'

As they seemed a nice enough couple, I decided to come clean and admit to being the Right Honourable Jeremy Corbyn MP, Leader of Her Majesty's Opposition.

Deborah said: 'Blimey, he is and all!'

Glenn said: 'Sorry, mate, we're not really into all that politics crap. Gets on me bloody tits, if I'm honest.'

I confessed that I feel much the same way – in fact, this was largely the basis for my going on holiday.

Glenn said: 'Tell me about it! I'm in bathroom supplies and a couple of weeks ago I thought: "If I see another urinal cake I'm gonna scream."'

We continued chatting in this vein for a while, before I realised I should be getting back to my wife.

However, we agreed it would be lovely to meet up at some point, so I gave them the address of our villa.

Later, walking through the city centre, I marvelled at all the exotic manhole covers, pointing out each and every one of them to Mrs Corbyn. A little after noon, we became peckish and so decided to stop at a typical Spanish *restaurante* (restaurant). I decided to order off menu, to make it clear that I'm a seasoned traveller and not some wide-eyed tourist. Mrs Corbyn settled on a potato omelette, while I opted for broken eggs. I approached the counter and introduced myself to the waiter.

I said: '*¡Hola! ¿Puedo tener la tortilla de patata y los huevos ranas, por favor?*'

The waiter blinked, then said: '*¿Huevos ranas?*'

I said: '*Si.*'

He said: 'This is not something we do, *señor.*'

I replied (in perfect Spanish) that I would appreciate it very much if *el cocinero* could sort some out for me.

He said: 'I really don't think you would like it ...'

This debate soon became heated, with me deploying some of my most strident vocabulary. Eventually Mrs Corbyn interceded, explaining that I had meant to order *huevos rotos* (broken eggs) rather than *huevos ranas*, which means frogspawn. Of course, I apologised to the waiter, but this error – which I'd say was rather minor – cast something of a pall over lunch. However, I soon cheered up when we walked past a stand selling vegan ice cream.

In the evening, we received a call from Glenn and Deborah and agreed to meet at a local watering hole called *La Barba Blanca*. They were delighted to be introduced to Mrs Corbyn and proceeded to order a cascade of *cervezas* and a tsunami of tequila. I became somewhat merry after drinking a 'virgin' mojito which I suspect may have had a couple of encounters round the back of the bike shed. Perhaps a little boisterously, I began to outline my core political philosophy. I said: 'The problem with Westminster is it's all about process, ritual, pointless bickering and public-school debate. That's not the kind of politics I believe in. Ultimately, what connects all of us is love. We've got to have more love in public life. Man or woman, rich or poor, black, white, gay or straight – everyone should just come together. We need to come together every day, in every possible combination!'

At this, Deborah gave my thigh a supportive squeeze and Glenn exclaimed: 'Jez, I don't care what the telly or the papers say – you're all right in my book!'

He and Deborah were keen for us to come back to their villa for a nightcap, but Mrs Corbyn and I were exhausted, so had to decline this kind offer. They really are the friendliest couple! How ironic that we had to travel to Spain to meet acceptable members of the British public ...

28th May

Mrs Corbyn and I decided to spend this morning on the beach. She was keen to get out there and swim in the sea and, as such, became rather restless when I spent half an hour applying suncream (SPF 100 – you can't be too careful with that kind of thing). Eventually we headed out and, as my darling wife splashed about in the surf, I decided to explore the shoreline. I was happily admiring some algae when suddenly a blinding pain shot up my leg. With a yelp, I looked down and saw that a small crab had gripped my toe in its pincer. Fortunately, I was able to shake it off before much damage was incurred.

I'm ashamed to say I nearly picked up a stone and smashed the thing, though I soon thought better of it. I said: 'Scuttle along, my cancrine comrade – I forgive you!'

Upon returning to the villa, I discovered that, in spite of my SPF 100, I had developed a markedly rosy complexion. While my wife has the resilience of her Mexican forebears, those born with the name Corbyn have a tendency to get sunstroke if they so much as turn on a lightbulb.

Around lunchtime, we made a Skype call to The Boy on Mrs Corbyn's iPad. As soon as he answered, I could tell from his expression and frazzled tone that something was wrong. He said: 'Okay, don't get cross, but El Gato was hungry, so I gave him some milk out of the fridge. Y'know, a bowl of milk – that's the classic meal for a cat, right?'

I said: 'Not poor old El Gato – he's lactose intolerant!'

He said: 'Well, I know that now, don't I? Anyway, he got some pretty serious diarrhoea and started running around the living room … Made a real mess.'

I let out a despairing moan. The Boy continued: 'Yeah, it's been pretty stressful, but now I've calmed him down and cleaned everything up, so you don't need to worry.' At this point he looked to one side, cried, 'Oh God, he's doing it again,' and ended the call abruptly.

Mrs Corbyn said: 'Well, at least he hasn't burned the house down …'

Spent the rest of the day sightseeing, then went over to Glenn and Deborah's rented villa for some drinks. I'm sorry to say that this was much less enjoyable than our previous evening together. Around 11 p.m., Deborah sat down beside Mrs Corbyn and began stroking her hair, while Glenn disappeared into the bedroom and emerged moments later wearing naught but a silk robe.

He said: 'All right, why don't the four of us get down to business?'

It emerges that husband and wife are part of the 'swinger' community and had, up to this point, laboured under the misapprehension that some wife-swapping was on the table. Now, I may be an open-minded individual – some of my best friends are pescatarian – but neither I nor my wife have ever taken any interest in that sort of thing. When I explained this, the convivial mood soured instantly. With a hurt look, Glenn said: 'I thought we were all on the same page. I mean, what about last night? You kept banging on about "sharing love" and "coming together" … Plus, you're a politician – all you guys are into kinky shit!'

An appalled Mrs Corbyn stormed out. I made my apologies, said that I hoped this wouldn't affect their voting intentions, then followed. Once back in our own villa, my wife and I vowed never to speak of the matter again.

29th May

I had thought I'd feel sad to be going home. However, after last night's hijinks, I was more than happy to vamoose. Without wishing to be ungrateful (travel is, after all, a bourgeois luxury), I feel less relaxed at the end of this holiday than I did before it …

After an uneventful flight, we found ourselves back in Gatwick, where a squall of British rain greeted us. While queuing for customs, it struck me how much faster the EU line is than the non-EU line. For the first time, I wondered if I should perhaps be doing more to avert Brexit …

Upon returning home, it became immediately apparent that The Boy's efforts to clean up after

El Gato had been only partially successful. Worse, I switched on my mobile to find that I'd received over 3,000 texts and 200 missed calls. I couldn't bring myself to listen to many of the voicemails, but one expletive-laden tirade from Tom Watson made it clear that my colleagues did not appreciate me going on an impromptu trip. Between this and the aforementioned queue speed disparity, I've decided I need to get my arse in gear …

Chapter Nine

The British public exercises its democratic right in the most baffling way possible. Lots of unnecessary rudeness. Basically everyone resigns except for me. A vote of no confidence serves to dent my confidence.

23rd June

Dear Diary, I'm sorry I haven't been more talkative over the past few weeks. I have been making Herculean efforts to get the Remain campaign back on track, while talking about Brexit nigh on every day. I'm absolutely shattered and my allotment is but a distant memory. Yet still I'm dogged by accusations that I don't care about the EU! Admittedly, I didn't help my case by going on *The Last Leg* and saying I was only seven, or seven and a half, out of ten in favour of remaining. But, I ask you, what politician could withstand the laser-like interview technique of comedian Adam Hills?

In truth, the last few weeks have been a terribly grim time in our nation's politics. The highlights (if that's quite the word) are as follows:

- Gove and Johnson unveiled a deceitful bus, adorned with claims that we send the EU £350 million a week, which we could be spending on the National Health Service. Naturally, I was horrified to see public transport misused like this. While I'm all for additional NHS funding, I don't believe for a second that Boris will be the one to provide it. If he had an extra £350 million, he'd use it for some vanity project, like a flying bridge or a skyscraper in the shape of his face.

- I refused to campaign alongside David Cameron, partly because I disagree with his vision of a globalised, free-market Europe and partly because he's a smarmy, gammon-hued tosspot.

- The Leave campaign dialled up its already considerable xenophobia. The dogwhistles were so loud that each canine in a twelve-mile radius suffered hearing loss. Perhaps the darkest point was when Nigel Farage was photographed in front of a poster depicting a column of brown-skinned refugees and claiming that Europe is at 'breaking point'. No, Nigel, the only thing that's at breaking point is your liver!

And so here it is: Referendum Day. It's been raining cats and dogs, which the folks in my office are worried will diminish turnout. It's certainly been diminishing my will to live!

I'm writing this in my office, around midnight, as we wait for the votes to come in. Everyone's terribly nervous, but I'm keeping a level head. The polling, punditry and expert advice all gives me confidence that Remain will prevail. More importantly than that, I understand the people of this country. The British are many things: stubborn; parochial; borderline alcoholic. But, more than anything, we are pragmatic. Tempers may flare and emotions run high, but in the end the British public will always take the most sensible path.

4 *a.m*: Oh dear ...

24th June

Today was something of a rollercoaster. Not an enjoyable one – more the kind that goes haywire and decapitates half the people riding it. Cameron has resigned! At least he'll now be able to spend more time playing Fruit Ninja on his iPad ...

Everyone on the radio sounds as though they're in shock. You half expect one of them to start sobbing and shout: 'I can't do this anymore! There's just too much news!'

Arrived at the Leader's Office to scenes of absolute chaos. Julian was rocking back and forth in his chair. I told him everything would be all right, to which he responded: 'But what if the economy crashes? I can't go back to living on my parents' estate!'

As I walked away, I heard someone mutter: 'Great job, Mr Seven Out Of Ten!'

I entered my office to find John McD waiting there. He said: 'Well, isn't this a delightful mess? The British public have put the "dumb" in "referendum".'

I said that we had to respect the democratic process and that there was a clear mandate for change. He said: '52 to 48? That's not a clear mandate for anything. The people have spoken, and they didn't make any sense!'

Gove and Johnson gave a press conference around 11 p.m. They may have won a historic victory, but you wouldn't know that to look at them. No, they had the demeanour of two teenage boys who'd just been caught molesting the family pet. It's almost as though they're a pair of posh chancers who wanted to boost their standing with weird Tory Europhobes, but never thought they'd have to deal with the reality of Brexit … Then again, who am I to question the integrity of notorious truth-teller Boris Johnson?

Had an emergency meeting with the Shadow Cabinet, at which a number of unkind things were said. As torrential rain drummed against the window, each of my colleagues took it in turns to lay into me. Now, I don't approve of swearing, so I will replace the saltier choices of vocabulary with 'thing':

> *'For thing's sake, Jeremy! You defended the EU with all the enthusiasm of a tortoise on Quaaludes.'*
>
> *'I can't decide what's thinging worse – your sixth-form political beliefs or your pre-school managerial skills.'*
>
> *'You've done more damage to the Labour Party than if someone put Margaret Thatcher's brain into an 80-foot killer robot with cannons for arms.'*
>
> *'I thinging hate you, you thinging piece of thing.'*

I responded to all this abuse by smiling politely and saying: 'That's an interesting point.' However, this only seemed to make things worse. Hilary Benn said: 'Look, Jeremy, you can't just sit there nodding. The country's thinged and it's your fault.'

I said: 'Now, that's hardly fair – I'm not the one who called a referendum.'

He said: 'Leave won by a stupidly small margin. Call me a romantic, but don't you think the result might have been different if the Leader of the Opposition hadn't campaigned with the air of someone about to have major dental surgery?'

There followed yet more sweeping criticism of my leadership style, ability to communicate and, in a couple of instances, appearance.

Owen Smith said: 'I suppose this is what you get when your leader cares more about growing marrows than securing votes ...'

I said: 'That's an interesting point.'

For some reason, this caused Hilary to leap across the table at me. Fortunately, he was restrained by Jon Trickett and Rachel Reeves. The meeting broke up soon afterwards.

25th June

According to today's papers, Hilary Benn is preparing a coup against me. I had no idea that Hilary would do such a thing – I mean, sure, he's always calling me unfit, useless and a liability to the Labour Party, but that's true of most of my colleagues. John McD reckons I have to fire him. He said: 'That way, anything he says sounds like sour grapes, rather than a principled stand.'

I replied that I'd rather not, given how I hate confrontation.

He said: 'Look, this is like a gangster movie. Anyone goes against the boss, they get whacked. *Capiche?*'

I said: 'Bless you.'

God, I hate the shouting, the intrigue, the *Godfather* references! I didn't get into politics to fire people. I've sacrificed so much for this job and all I get in return is relentless criticism. Still, I'm not going anywhere. Firstly, because I have a duty to represent the will of the membership. Secondly, because I want to spite these Blairite tossers ...

26th June

Was having a lovely dream about tractors when I was suddenly woken by the sound of my 'Solidarity Forever' ringtone. Glancing at the alarm clock, I saw that it was 1 a.m. My late-night caller turned out to be Hilary Benn, who said: 'I'm sorry, Jeremy, but I've lost confidence in your ability to lead the party.'

Well, it's news to me that he ever had confidence! I'd been dreading firing the guy, but after he wrenched me away from my dream, it was nothing less than a pleasure.

By the time I got to the Leader's Office, it became clear that Benn had orchestrated a string of resignations in the Shadow Cabinet. They were falling like a bunch of centrist dominos: first Heidi Alexander, then Gloria De Piero, then Ian Murray ... It soon became quicker to list the ministers who hadn't resigned. I told Julian that I urgently needed to speak to my deputy. He said: 'No can do – Tom's at Glastonbury. Apparently someone just photographed him dancing at a silent disco.'

Spent the rest of the day frantically appointing new ministers to fill all the vacancies. The mood in the office is glummer than ever. John said: 'We're promoting people I've never heard of! If we keep going at this rate, the Shadow Cabinet's going to consist of Ken Livingstone, the Cheeky Girls and a cardboard cut-out of Scrappy Doo.'

I tried to lighten spirits with a witticism: 'Our cabinet has fallen apart so quickly, you'd think we bought it from IKEA!' This, it emerged, was insufficient to cut through the gloom, so I tried another: 'You could say that the Shadow Cabinet is a *shadow* of its former self!'

John said: 'All right, Jez, enough of the stand-up routine. I'd tell you not to quit your day job, but soon that might not be a choice.'

I smiled sheepishly and offered to get everyone tea.

When I came home, I was determined to make something of a uniformly terrible day, so wrote the following:

WOBBLY CABINET
By Jeremy Corbyn

The Labour folks moderate and Blairite
Are thundering with all of their might.
They stomp and they mutter, they curse and they frown

Tell papers it's worse than it was under Brown,
And what should the source of their terror be
But a bearded old fella called Jeremy?
They call me inept, does this silly band.
Well, how am I lamer than Ed Miliband?
It's really about our political persuasions
Therefore I'm resigned to their resignations.

27th June

Commons back from recess. Ran into David Cameron in the Royal Gallery. I had expected him to be somewhat chastened by recent events, but he looked as smug and shiny as usual. I said: 'David, I hope you're keeping well, all things considered.'

He said: 'Oh God, yes! Losing that referendum is the best thing that ever happened to me! Now I can chillax 24/7 and enjoy being a very rich man.'

I frowned, observing that, throughout the campaign, he had argued that Brexit would do huge damage to the country. Cameron said: 'Probably, but who cares? Even if Britain turns into a *Mad Max*-style dystopia, I can always buy a fortress or something.'

Though I have never had what you would call a high opinion of the man, this shocked me nonetheless. It must have shown on my face, because he proceeded to say: 'Come on, Jezza, it's not like you can get on your high horse – you basically did sod-all. Anyway, I'd say *au revoir*, but one of the benefits of retirement is that I'll never have to interact with oiks like you again.'

With that, he slapped me on the back and walked away, pausing only to apply some antibacterial gel to his hand.

28th June

A motion of no confidence in my leadership has been passed by 172 Labour MPs to 40. I must admit, this isn't the sort of pick-me-up I need at the moment. I've withstood the pressure to resign thus far because the PLP didn't elect me, the membership did. They could have chosen some slick New Labour droid who'd make the same brutal cuts as the Tories, but look a bit sad while doing it. Instead, they chose me, warts and all. But what if I am unfit? What if the media, political commentators, most of my colleagues and a majority of the country are right? I certainly never expected to be leader of the Labour Party, so it shouldn't be a surprise that other people find it strange. Between you and me, dear Diary, I was feeling a bit shaky by the end of the day.

However, as unfortunate as I may be in terms of colleagues, I am profoundly fortunate in the family with which I've been blessed. As soon as I came in the front door, they could tell that my travails were weighing heavily upon me. Mrs Corbyn gave me a hug and said: 'I don't care what those *pendejos* say – you're a kind and decent man and Labour's lucky to have you.'

The Boy said: 'I mean, yes, you're a bit of a disaster, but look at the alternatives. A bunch of empty suits who think the way to beat the Tories is to act like a Margaret Thatcher cover band!' They then showed incredible kindness by baking me a rhubarb crumble and letting me talk about the Viet Cong's use of bicycles for a whole hour.

As much as I appreciated their support, I still felt pretty blue while donning my pyjamas. I thought I'd try and cheer myself up by attempting a limerick:

LIMERICK #1
By Jeremy Corbyn

The whole Shadow Cabinet's resigned
Because I'm too leftward inclined.
They call me unfit
(Or else 'f–ing shit'),
But personally I don't believe that kind of name-calling
has any place in our politics.

Hmm, I may need more practice …

Chapter Ten

The Tories have a vigorous backstabbing contest. Angela Eagle launches a leadership challenge, then Owen Smith wades in. Theresa May becomes prime minister, largely due to the efforts of her opponents.

29th June

One Stephen Crabb has launched his campaign for the Tory leadership. Who the hell's this Crabb guy? I've been in Parliament for thirty-three years and I've never heard of him. Did a bit of research and wasn't at all impressed. He's horrifically right wing and a Christian fundamentalist, but what I *can't* forgive is his beard, which is a disgrace to all facial hair. It looks like a child drew it on with a stencil!

30th June

Johnson is out of the Tory leadership campaign! In a shocking act of blue-on-blue violence, Michael Gove announced this morning that Boris isn't up to the job and that he will be running himself. As fate would have it, I bumped into the former Mayor of London while I was walking round Westminster. He looked notably green around the gills, so I asked if he was feeling all right. He said: 'What do you think? Gove stitched me up like a kipper that just had open heart surgery. I was so depressed this morning I barely had the energy to mess up my hair.'

I was surprised to find that I felt sorry for Boris, in a fleeting sort of way. Since he was a toddler, all he's wanted was to prance around being prime minister. Now, having driven the country off a cliff, he's not only fallen at the first hurdle but somehow managed to impale himself on it. Still, I can't say I'm doing much better – the papers are full of Labour MPs briefing against me and talking about a leadership challenge. I'm finding leadership a challenge as it is!

2nd July

A strange, but rather exciting, dream: it was a sort of Hollywood action film with me as the protagonist. Wearing a dirty vest like Bruce Willis in *Die Hard*, I strode into the Commons, which was filled with villainous Blairites and Tories. They all jeered and, as I reached the despatch box, one of them stood up and said: 'Jeremy Corbyn! You've got some nerve coming in here, you old Trot. What do you want?'

I raised an eyebrow and, as cool as you like, replied: 'I came to kick ass and nationalise utilities. And I've nationalised all the utilities ...'

The MP laughed and said: 'What? But you're a puny peacenik! We moneyed elites won't go down without a fight.'

I said: 'Then it's time to put the "fist" in "pacifist",' and knocked him out with one punch. There was a posh screech and suddenly I saw Boris Johnson and Jacob Rees-Mogg coming at me, dressed as seventeenth-century royalists and wielding rapiers. I pulled out my trusty hammer and sickle and made short work of them. Then, using vegan karate, I dispatched the rest of the neoliberal horde. The last to fall was David Cameron, who begged for his life. He said: 'Please, Jeremy, have mercy! I promise I'll change my ways! I'll read the Communist Manifesto! Look, I'm sorry for making fun of you. I was jealous of your nice suits and cool beard!'

I just growled, 'This is for the workers,' and threw him out of a window and into the Thames.

When the smoke cleared, a beautiful young woman approached and said: 'Jeremy, I represent the People. We're all very impressed with your bravery and would be honoured if you agreed to be our king.'

I said that, as much as I appreciated the gesture, I am implacably opposed to the monarchy and, in any case, am far too humble to accept such a role. At this point, Che Guevara appeared beside me and patted me on the back. He said: 'You're doing a bang-up job, mate – don't let anyone tell you different.'

I awoke with a smile on my face, a little disappointed that it hadn't been real.

4th July

Today Nigel Farage resigned as UKIP leader for the third time. Makes sense, given how keen he is on exiting things. That said, it seems a bit suspicious that all the prominent Leave campaigners jumped ship as soon as Brexit became a reality. It's as though the head lemming decided, while his mates were cascading over the cliff, that he had too much to live for.

5th July

Stephen Crabb has withdrawn from the Tory leadership race after coming second-to-last in the first ballot. It would seem that the Crabb campaign went sideways. Ha! Ha! Ha!

7th July

Now Gove's out! I'm glad I won't be facing that creepy little swot at PMQs – he'd only have challenged me on arithmetic and Latin conjugations. It seems the Tory leadership will fall to either Theresa May (polite fascist) or someone called Andrea Leadsom (animatronic headmistress).

11th July

Spent all morning and much of last night researching Andrea Leadsom who, I'm told, could pull off an upset and pip May to the post. I can comfortably say I'm now one of the world's foremost Leadsom experts, having become intimately acquainted with her Aylesbury upbringing, her career as a debt trader, and the ways in which her devout Christianity has informed her political views.

Later: Leadsom dropped out. Brilliant ... Congratulations to Theresa May, who has become prime minister despite no one actually liking her. She must be delighted that her opponents chose to combine the final scene of *Hamlet* with a Three Stooges film.

Later still: Perhaps I shouldn't have indulged in the above *schadenfreude* (if you're even allowed to use such words in Brexit Britain). Angela Eagle has announced a challenge to my leadership, with Owen Smith following close behind, like a terrier nipping at her heels. Presumably they will now duke it out to see who should be my moderate opponent. How exciting: two moderates trying to out-moderate each other, a real clash of the average-sized ...

THERESA MAY

Was so fed up by the time I got home, I entirely lacked the energy to make dinner. However, Mrs Corbyn whipped up some delicious vegetarian quesadillas. I should let her cook more often!

13th July

Watched Theresa May's speech upon entering Downing Street. It was all about 'fairness' and 'opportunity', which she will presumably achieve by further slashing the welfare state, deregulating the banks and deporting anyone with so much as a suntan. Back when she was Home Secretary, she approved a scheme where a series of vans drove around London with billboards reading 'In the UK illegally? Go home or face arrest.' What is it with Tories and putting horrible statements on motor vehicles? Anyway, the only part of the speech that struck a chord was when she talked about job insecurity – I very much know the feeling …

In other news, The Boy has been moved from the Comms Office to the Grassroots Outreach Unit, where – in the words of his manager – he can 'do less immediate damage'. Over dinner, I quizzed him about what had gone wrong. He said: 'I made a lot of enemies in Comms. You tell a few people that what they're doing is rubbish and all of a sudden they want to show you the door.'

I advised him to be less provocative in his new role, as I have always found it helpful to be quiet and self-effacing. He replied: 'That's all well and good, Dad, but literally everyone you work with wants to get rid of you!'

Sometimes I don't know why I bother ...

Chapter Eleven

Eagle drops out, leaving me to face an aggressive Welshman. I am forced to travel around the country in order to keep my job. Yet another unsatisfactory train journey, this time with repercussions. I spend a harrowing night in Newcastle.

14th July

Had a run-in with Owen Smith in the Portcullis Cafeteria. He walked in and assumed a stance that was no doubt intended to be powerful (chin jutting, chest thrust out, feet about a metre apart). Unfortunately, it looked as though he'd forgotten to take the coat hanger out of his jacket. Upon spotting me, he boomed: 'All right Jezza?'

I said: 'Hello, Owen.'

He said: 'What's that supposed to mean? Here, are you having a go?'

I replied that I meant no offence. He said: 'Now, look you, boyo! Better watch yourself, yeah? You may have beaten Yvette and that lot, but you've never had to throw down with the O-Dogg.'

When I expressed the view that there was no need for us to antagonise each other, he observed that I had no idea how hated I am among my MPs. He said: 'If you think what they say in the press is bad, you should hear what they say behind closed doors.'

I said: 'Well, it's all just politics, isn't it?'

He said: 'Yes! And we're bloody politicians!'

I suppose he's got me there.

19th July

Today the Leader's Office received word that Angela Eagle has dropped out of the leadership race, in order to give Owen a clear shot at toppling me. Spying the chance for some levity, I remarked: 'I guess you could say the Eagle has *crash-landed*!'

John McD replied, rather unkindly: 'Yes, Jeremy, you *could* say that, but you definitely shouldn't.'

21st July

In a development that makes UK politics seem somewhat less insane, Donald Trump has officially been named Republican nominee for president. Donald Trump! That Frankenstein's monster of American capitalism! A McDonald's cheeseburger come to life! The poor man's version of Alan Sugar! Watching Trump bluster and mug his way through interviews, it occurred to me that the guy has a touch of Boris about him. Not just the ludicrous blond nest on his head, but also that oily sense of entitlement. In any case, the guy represents everything I hate about America, the West and the world in general (though he does have a point about lying journalists and fake news).

Today also saw the first hustings of the leadership challenge. Owen and I faced off in Cardiff, which I initially thought would give him a home advantage, but no. It seemed as though his tie was cutting off the circulation to his head. Afterwards, I asked Julian how he thought it had gone. He said: 'Yeah, you were great during the bits I was awake for.'

I'm writing this in a fairly depressing Travelodge, miles from the city centre. My room commands a majestic view of the refuse area and the trouser press is prohibitively temperamental. Oh, how I yearn for my beloved Islington! Was cheered somewhat by a call from Mrs Corbyn and The Boy. Apparently my son is enjoying his new role in the Grassroots Outreach Unit. He said: 'It's brilliant – literally no one has any idea what we're meant to be doing, so we just spend all day reading *Vice* and watching YouTube compilations!'

If I wasn't so firmly committed to workers' rights, I might have something to say about that ...

11th August

Once again, I must apologise for the egregious gap between entries. To be honest, I've been at something of a low ebb recently, and not much inclined to record my experiences. However, this was changed today by a truly appalling train journey (I suppose that's one thing Chris Grayling's accomplished!). While travelling up to Gateshead for a leadership hustings, I had the misfortune to find myself dealing with Virgin. Through typical capitalist greed, the train had been totally overbooked, with not a free seat to be found. After fruitlessly wandering through several carriages, I was forced to sit on the floor, uncomfortably close to a bin.

THE TRAIN

As I languished there, trying to ignore the stench whenever the toilet door slid open, I felt the poetic muse come upon me. I believe it was Wordsworth who said that poetry 'takes its origin from emotion recollected in tranquillity'. Well, with all due respect, I wrote this while fuming on the floor of a Virgin train:

RAM-PACKED
By Jeremy Corbyn

We've all gone off the rails,
We're in a mess, a Branson pickle,
Sardined in squalor, sweating,
The buffet car is out of vegan wraps.
A desert of commutered seats
With no oasis for the weary arse,
Therefore I sit upon the floor
And weep.
They're cross in King's Cross.
They've gone mental in Glasgow Central.
Clapham Junction's ceased to function.
I'm dreading my trip to Reading.
Yet still, on top of this
Are ticket prices surgin'

So, though it seems a paradox,
You've really screwed us, Virgin.
Renationalise the railways!
Renationalise the railways!
RENATIONALISE THE RAILWAYS!

As I read these words back, I decided the general public had a right to know about my horrific treatment. Having instructed Julian to record me on his phone, I came out with the following: 'This is a problem that many passengers face every day on the trains: commuters and long-distance travellers. Today this train is completely ram-packed. The reality is there's not enough trains, we need more of them. And they're also incredibly expensive. Isn't that a good case for public ownership?'

Stirring words, I'm sure you'll agree, and all off the top of my head. Julian observed that he'd never heard the phrase 'ram-packed' and asked whether I meant to say 'jam-packed'.

I replied: 'No, I would never associate jam with something negative.'

Later: Hustings was the usual sort of thing: Owen saying that he's more electable than me, despite looking like an accountant who describes himself as the 'office legend'. Afterwards, I stepped out of the venue for a breath of fresh air. To my surprise, I was hailed by a group of Geordie gentlemen who were clearly in an advanced stage of drunkenness. 'Fook me, it's that Jeremy Corbyn off of the telly!' said one of them.

'Aye, it fookin' is, like!' said another.

The third, who I would come to know as Gaz, said: 'How, Jezza, mate! Wanna gan oot on the town and get lashed?'

As a man of the people, I felt I had to oblige. What followed was a night that I would love to forget, but fear I never shall. I saw tattooed men brawling outside kebab shops in the Bigg Market. Scantily clad young women crawling down Northumberland Street amid rivers of urine. A bloke wearing a traffic cone on his head, who walked up to a police horse and knocked it out with a single punch. All these elements merged into a vomit-flecked kaleidoscope as I witnessed intoxication, depravity and wanton destruction on a scale I'm unable to describe. It was as though Hieronymus Bosch had been tasked with depicting an especially rowdy Wetherspoons.

I asked Gaz whether he'd ever seen anything like it. He replied: 'Standard Thursday night.'

Some call New York 'the city that never sleeps'. Based on what I saw today, Newcastle should be known as 'the city that passes out' …

Chapter Twelve

Another troublesome development regarding The Boy. Constituency work and a canine misadventure. I retain my position, if not my joie de vivre.

15th August

Suffered a real blow today – The Boy has been sacked from the Grassroots Outreach Unit!

Apparently he took the department's *laissez-faire* attitude to work too far. He said: 'I thought I'd be fine, what with my dad being leader and all, but it turns out they really don't respect you!'

To my chagrin, The Boy seems entirely unperturbed by this development and is happy to spend his time cavorting around country houses with Anunciata. That girl is having a bad influence on him – he actually referred to me as 'Pa-paaaah' the other day! Upon seeing the change in my expression, he apologised and corrected himself to 'Dad'. If he starts wearing a cravat, I don't know what I'll do ...

Spent much of the day in surgery, meeting with the constituents of Islington North. While more careerist MPs may find it a drag, this is among my favourite parts of the job. Hearing the hopes, fears and concerns of neighbours keeps me connected to ordinary life and reminds me why I went into politics. Obviously, most of the people who come to see you are weird malcontents, but one has a duty to represent them too.

Had one slightly awkward meeting, in which a lady called Patricia complained about dogs 'running wild' on the streets of Highbury. She proposed that I introduce legislation to require all dogs be kept on a leash. I told her – very politely – that I could never support such a policy, as canines have just as much right to roam free as humans. When I refused to back down on this point, she became agitated and furnished me with some choice words ('leftie ponce', etc.) before departing. This is unfortunate, but, then again, I've got one of the safest seats in the country, so I can afford to annoy a few people!

THE DOG

16th August

Was cycling through Highbury this morning when a small dog came bounding across my path. I swerved violently, which almost caused me to collide with an organic burrito stall. The woman manning it (womanning it?) yelled: 'Oi, Jeremy, learn how to ride a bike!'

This hair-raising experience forced me not only to swerve, but to make a U-turn on the dog-leash issue. It turns out Patricia had a very decent point (apart from calling me a ponce) and I will begin drafting legislation ASAP. I think it's important that leaders be flexible in their thinking. The supple reed may bend where the mighty oak would fall!

18th August

Hustings in Nottingham. Owen was asked what my best quality is and replied, with a smirk: 'He's got a very nice line in cream suits.'

Now, as a pacifist both politically and personally, I take great pride in my self-control. However, at that moment, I couldn't help but fantasise about strangling the goon with his own tie. You don't go

after a man's cream suits. That just isn't something
you do.

9th September

Owen Smith has given an interview saying that
he fought off 'hundreds of lads' to get his wife,
thus proving that he knows how to win. Big deal!
I persuaded three different women to marry me,
despite the fact I only buy four pairs of underwear
per decade!

12th September

The first anniversary of becoming leader. I'm celebrating in a soulless hotel room in Swindon, as I dot
from town to town, fighting to keep my job. I doubt
Paperchase has a card for this particular situation.

14th September

Back in the Leader's Office, between endless, pointless hustings. While making some herbal tea for
the IT guys, I overheard a conversation between
John and Diane. He was saying: 'Look, I need you

out there, doing more interviews in support of Jeremy.'

She expressed a great deal of reluctance, adding: 'What am I meant to say when they ask if he's electable? Or whether I trust his judgement? We both know I'm very fond of Jeremy, but the guy could get lost in a compass factory!'

With friends like these ...

17th September

Another debate against Owen Smith, in Glasgow this time. By now the pattern is well established. First question: 'Mr Corbyn, a lot of people say that you're rubbish. Do you agree?' Second question: 'Mr Smith, would you agree that Mr Corbyn is rubbish?' Despite this blatant preferential treatment, Owen still manages to be about as inspiring as a flat tyre. When asked about our key policy differences, he said (I'm paraphrasing): 'I like all of the things people like Jeremy for liking, except I like them in a more electable way. I'm secretly a massive socialist, but I'm also a sexy vote-magnet. So, if you want Jeremy Corbyn, you should definitely vote for Owen Smith.'

Another debate, another Travelodge. While lying in my hotel bed this evening, it occurred to me to watch a film on pay-per-view. However, as the only options were *The King's Speech* and *Despicable Me 2*, I decided to call The Boy instead. His job search was not going well, he said: 'You know what it's like, what with austerity and the credit crunch ... It's basically impossible to find a decent job where you can work seven hours a day tops.'

I responded that it must be tough being unemployed. He said: 'Not really – I'm having a great time. Nun and I just got really into water polo! Plus, it's great to be away from Labour HQ – that place is so depressing.'

After the last couple of months, I can't say I disagree!

24th September

The whole sorry business of this leadership challenge drew to a close today, as I was re-elected leader with 62 per cent of the vote. When my opponent and I were given the results before the announcement, I said: 'Look, Owen, I appreciate that this has been a difficult few months for everyone concerned, but I hope we can now work together to make this country a better place.'

He turned to me with a face like thunder and said: 'Fat chance! You may have turned Labour into your own weird little cult, but good luck winning an election!'

And so ended a thoroughly unimpressive coup. Honestly, it was like the assassination of Julius Caesar, if Brutus et al had been wielding plastic spoons.

As I walked on stage to give my victory speech, I could hear hundreds of people chanting 'JEZ WE CAN! JEZ WE CAN!' I looked out into the crowd and saw a sea of hopeful faces gazing back at me, cheering in spite of all this rancour and kerfuffle. That's something, I suppose. Still, I can't claim to be particularly happy. Over the last couple of months, I've been forced to squander tremendous amounts of energy that could have gone on more important things, like cultivating maize or re-grouting the downstairs bathroom. And bringing down this Tory government, of course.

Chapter Thirteen

*My second party conference as leader. The Boy
has some capitalist notions. All eyes on America.
Once more, the unthinkable happens. The most
unpleasant phone call of my life.*

26th September

Conference time again, which means I have the
great pleasure of spending a few days in Liverpool
with hundreds of people who hate me. Nothing
too interesting to report, except for a worrying
phone conversation with The Boy. I asked whether
he was having any luck on the job front yet. He
said: 'Not exactly, but there's been one exciting
development ...'

Apparently he's keen to get into the tech industry, having had an idea for a 'really cool app'. He
said: 'I just need to find someone who can code and

some people to market it, then *boom* – I'm sorted for life.'

The 'City lads' have all promised to invest, as have Anunciata's parents. I asked what exactly this app would *do*, to which he replied: 'Never mind – it would just go over your head!'

It's true that I've always been something of a technophobe – I only consented to getting a MySpace account last year – but still, I don't want my son associating with those dreadful Silicon Valley types. To help steer him in the right direction, I thought I'd make a list of jobs I consider to be morally acceptable:

- Miner, factory guy, etc.
- Proprietor of a boutique knitwear store
- Working at the RSPB
- Vegan butcher, AKA gardener
- Unsuccessful musician
- Journalist for the *Morning Star*
- Street performer, esp. living statue
- Labour MP (as a last resort)

Texted this to The Boy. No reply so far – strange, given he's always on his phone.

27th September

Yesterday was the first presidential debate between Hillary Clinton and Donald Trump, which I didn't watch. Can't say I'm particularly happy about either candidate – one of them is a right-wing, authoritarian, warmongering shill for big business, and the other is Donald Trump. I do wish Bernie Sanders had got the Democratic nomination. There's something I like about that white-haired socialist who's spent his whole career in the political wilderness, but I can't put my finger on it.

2nd October

Today Theresa May gave her speech to the Tory conference in Birmingham. It was the usual nonsense: platitudes about 'fairness' and 'opportunity' mixed with deranged right-wing policies. Her big treat for the grassroots is a pledge to make British soldiers exempt from human rights legislation during combat. When else would those laws be necessary – while they're in the shower? I mean really … She might as well make it legal to hunt foxes with air-to-surface missiles.

As ever, the Tory delegates were the only thing of interest (by which I mean, scientific interest). Their average age is 'dead for a decade' and anyone under thirty looks like they're impersonating Billy Bunter. I can just about understand people who vote Conservative – they're just greedy and heartless. However, my mind reels at the psychosexual pathology that would compel one to attend a talk by Liam Fox ...

7th October

This morning the office was flooded with giggles and gasps of disbelief. Julian ran up to me and, proffering his smartphone, exclaimed: 'Trump's messed up this time, even by his standards!'

It seems the orange fiend has been caught on tape bragging to the host of *Access Hollywood* about his history of sexual assault. The presenter in question is Billy Bush, whose family are responsible for CIA atrocities and the near total disintegration of the Middle East. It's quite a feat to look worse than a member of that detestable brood, but Donald has certainly managed.

Julian said: 'I mean, that's it, right? There's no way he can come back from this. Who in their right mind would vote for him?'

I said that it was never wise to bet against the American public doing the most abhorrent thing possible. Still, I granted, a Trump victory seems unlikely. Julian said: 'Yeah, even before this tape, his approval ratings were in the gutter. Polls don't lie.'

After a beat, he looked alarmed and said: 'Except the ones about you!'

I must admit the Trump footage disturbed me. While I find it hard to be shocked by a country whose politics produced Ronald Reagan and George W. Bush, the man is remarkably unpleasant. I would never so much as wink at a female comrade, let alone 'grab them by the pussy'! Speaking of which, I better fetch El Gato in from the garden.

4th November

Yesterday, the High Court ruled that only Parliament, not the government, has the power to 'trigger Article 50' (I've no idea what Article 50 is, but it seems to involve Europe). The response from certain elements of the press has been predictably demented – today the *Daily Mail* ran mugshots of the offending judges, under the headline ENEMIES OF THE PEOPLE. That's pretty rich – if anyone's an enemy of the people, it's the *Mail*'s editor, Paul Dacre.

I was appalled by this cynical attack and felt compelled to write the following:

An Ode to Paul Dacre
By Jeremy Corbyn

Mister Paul Dacre,
The awful muckraker,
The foul money-maker
And total piss-taker.
When I see Paul Dacre
I run for an acre,
If my wife read the Mail
I'd have to forsake her.
We all know Paul Dacre's
A rake and a faker,
A front-page half-baker
And truth's undertaker.
In fact, he's a villain,

A bigger lawbreaker
Than Drax, the main bad guy
In Bond film Moonraker.

Looking back through these pages, I see my poems are starting to pile up! Soon I'll have enough for a collection – a chapbook at the very least. Must tell Julian to get in touch with Faber & Faber.

8th November

Today is the US presidential election, so the news is all America, all the time. I can't say I understand this whole 'Special Relationship' thing. I suspect it has more to do with us being too lazy to learn other languages than anything else. What do we really have in common with a place where they give you a free assault rifle with every McRib and socialism is considered a faux pas on the level of pet necrophilia? A country that has – uniquely in human history – dropped nuclear bombs on another nation, and yet still views itself as the world's moral leader? A place where Henry Kissinger is a respected elder statesman, rather than someone kept in stocks and taken from town to town so that the locals can hurl decomposing produce at him? On the other hand, I once enjoyed a nice trip to Florida, so swings and roundabouts.

Decided to have an early night, as Hillary Clinton seems to have this one in the bag. After all, this Trump is a moral abomination and a blatant buffoon. No country would elect him, not even America!

9th November

Arrived at the office to find everyone white-faced, teary-eyed and shaking their heads in disbelief. I often see my staff like that, but not so early in the day. I asked what the matter was and Julian switched on the TV, which showed the Donald grinning orangely at his victory party. After a long pause, I tried to cheer everyone up by suggesting they look on the bright side – such an appalling failure of the neoliberal status quo might well hasten its demise. That is, unless Trump starts a nuclear war and annihilates us all. I'm not sure to what extent my contribution helped.

Later: Good God, though!

THE US ELECTION RESULT

11th November

Julian tells me that President-elect Trump would like to have an official phone call with me, as Leader of Her Majesty's Opposition. Naturally I told him I would on no account speak to the man. He's a racist, an Islamophobe, an alleged sex criminal and, worst of all, a businessman. John said: 'For God's sake, Jeremy, it's basic diplomacy! What if you end up becoming PM?'

Sally said: 'After the other night, the idea doesn't seem quite so ludicrous.'

I choose to take this as encouragement, rather than a slight. In any case, I held firm.

Later: Mrs Corbyn being out with friends, I had free rein in matters culinary this evening. As such, I decided to treat myself with one my favourite recipes: baked beans with the sauce rinsed off. I was just about to tuck in when the phone started ringing. I was surprised, having made it perfectly clear to my comrades in the office that I would prefer not to be bothered with work stuff after six.

I answered to hear a familiar growl: 'Jared, how many more of these calls do I have to make? I'm sick of talking to dumbass foreigners. Most of them aren't even rich ...'

I said: 'Hello, this is Jeremy.'

The voice said: 'Yes, very good, this is President-elect Donald J. Trump. It's a yuge honour for you to be speaking to me. We're supposed to talk in case you get made King of England or whatever.'

I said: 'With all due respect, sir, I'd like to know how you got my home phone number.'

He said: 'Oh, it was easy. Now that I won the election, the CIA gets me any number I want. It's unbelievable – I told them to bug Kate Upton's apartment and they did it the next day.'

I said: 'I see. Well, perhaps we could talk about our respective policy positions?'

He replied: 'Positions? I've done all the positions. You know, back in the Eighties, I could have had any model I wanted. Cheryl Tiegs, Cindy Crawford ... If you talk to Elle Macpherson, don't listen to a word she says – I turned *her* down, okay?'

I said: 'Forgive me, Mr Trump, but I don't see how that's relevant to relations between the US and the UK.'

He said: 'Yes, very special relations. I love Britain. So loyal. You guys do whatever we tell you.

It's like we're Batman and you're our gay butler. I mean, Eye-rack? Unbelievable.'

I said: 'Actually, I'm proud to say I was a vehement opponent of the invasion of Iraq.'

He said: 'To be honest, I forget whether I was for it or against it, but still, you've got to admit, that war did kill a lot of terrorists. Or, at least, terrorist-looking people. And these guys, they're coming over. They're bringing drugs, they're bringing crime – not good. Trump's gonna secure our borders, believe me. Keep the Mexicans out.'

I said: 'I'll have you know that my wife is Mexican.'

He said: 'Hey, I'm fine with immigrants when they have sex with you, okay? My wife, Melania – beautiful woman – she's from Slovakia or Hungary or some other loser country. But most of these guys? Horrible. I mean, you live in London, right? That place is a war zone nowadays. You can't go out on your penny-farthing without getting shot or 9/11-ed – I saw it on Fox.'

I said: 'Firstly, you don't know a single thing about London. Secondly, I find your comments extremely racist.'

THE PHONECALL

He replied: 'FAKE NOOS! How can I be a racist? I let my daughter marry a Jew, and they're the sneakiest people around … You know Ivanka? Gorgeous girl. Amazing figure, easily a ten. Makes Melania look like crap, if I'm honest. God, if I wasn't her father …'

Now, I like to think I'm a pragmatic guy, but even I have my limits. After this barrage of grotesquerie, I needed to speak my mind. With a tone of righteous indignation, I said: 'Right, I can't keep this to myself any longer. You, sir, are the greatest charlatan I've ever encountered!'

He replied, without so much as a pause: 'Thanks, I appreciate that very much, I *am* the greatest. A tremendous charlatan, the world's leading charlatan. Many people are saying, Trump, he's the best who ever charlataned.' Seconds passed, then he said: 'Okay, Gerald, this has been great, but I like to watch five or six hours of TV a day, so I'd better go. Good luck with all the things you're doing, like playing soccer and toasting crumpets and whatnot. Say hi to Princess Diana from me.'

With that, he hung up. I returned to the table but was unable to finish my meal – the sauceless beans turned to ashes in my mouth.

13th November

In the sort of surreal happening that seems to occur every other day now, Nigel Farage has become the first British politician to meet with Trump, post-election. Julian showed me a picture of the pair grinning in front of a golden lift. It was quite possibly the most hideous photo I've seen in my entire life. How can so much vileness be contained in one tacky building? You would have thought they'd be afraid to stand next to each other, lest they collapse into a black hole of fascism.

Found myself fantasising about a revolution in America, with the new, leftist government seizing everything Trump owns. They would dismantle his tower brick by brick, then melt down all the gold to distribute among the working class. They could even burn that dreadful wig of his to keep a poor family warm! It pains me to speak ill of anyone, given that I am a humanist and believe that every individual should be treated with dignity and compassion. This being said, if I could flick a switch to send Trump and Farage plummeting nude down a mountain of nettles and syringes, I'd be hard-pressed to resist.

Chapter Fourteen

I favour The Boy with some romantic advice. The UK forgets its lines on the international stage. We have a disastrous dinner with Ms Anunciata Basildon-Wyck. A somewhat frosty Christmas.

3rd December

The Boy seemed unusually circumspect over breakfast, so I asked him what was up. He explained that funding has stalled for this much-heralded app of his. He said: 'Investors are so jittery at the moment. You tell them that you don't quite have a prototype or a business plan or a name for the thing and – whoosh – they head for the hills.'

I was about to launch into an anti-capitalist tirade when he cut me off, saying: 'I just want to impress Nun, you know? Show that I can be dependable, provide for her.'

I said: 'Take it from me, women aren't impressed by money and success. They care about more important things, like a commitment to hobbies and how many demonstrations you go on.'

He said: 'I'm not sure that's true at all.'

I said: 'Son, I've been married three times, so I think I know a thing or two about pleasing women. If you want to show this girl you're serious, give her a cute pet name, like "comrade". Or whisper sweet nothings about the renationalisation of water utilities.'

He told me my advice had been incredibly useful and that he would go and implement it right away. More top parenting from the Corbster!

8th December

It seems our illustrious Foreign Secretary has run into trouble again. Incidentally, it never stops being surreal that Boris Johnson, of all people, is responsible for our country's diplomacy. This is a man who has compared the EU to Hitler, written an obscene limerick about the President of Turkey and referred to African members of the Commonwealth as 'flag-waving piccaninnies'. As I see it, the PM might as well have gone the whole hog and given the job to Jim Davidson.

Anyway, Boris got slapped down by Downing Street for saying that Saudi Arabia is waging proxy wars in the Middle East. Rather ironic that the one time he tells the truth, he gets told off for it! We can't go admitting our allies are bloodthirsty tyrants, after all – how would we keep selling them billions of pounds' worth of weaponry?

15th December

A leaked memo by Sir Ivan Rogers, the UK's Permanent Representative to the European Union, estimates that reaching a deal with that organisation, post-Brexit, might take ten years. Imagine that – no deal until 2026! I'll be seventy-seven by then. I wonder if I'll still be leader of the Labour party ...

16th December

After a period of some eight months, The Boy finally consented to us meeting his girlfriend. Over breakfast, he blithely mentioned that Anunciata was free that evening, and could she possibly swing by? I asked him why exactly this has taken such a long time. He said: 'Well, Dad, you don't always make a great first impression. But things are serious enough now that I don't think there's much you could do to screw it up.'

I chose to ignore his customary rudeness and set about preparing for dinner. Mrs Corbyn insisted upon doing the cooking, so my *tofu á l'orange* will have to debut another day. I must confess I felt quite nervous to meet Ms Basildon-Wyck. The Boy is exceptionally keen on her and I didn't want to do or say anything that might cause him problems. After all, he sulked for days when I initially cautioned against an interclass coupling. I decided I should do some research, so went to my local newsagents and sheepishly bought a copy of *Tatler*, before conceal-ing it within my usual *Morning Star*. As loath as I am to give money to the proprietors of that maga-zine, I needed some insight into the upper-class mind, and I wasn't going to binge-watch *Downton Abbey*. I thought for a second that a comrade from our CLP had spotted me, but I was doubtless being paranoid.

Around 7:30 p.m. the doorbell sounded, nearly causing The Boy to jump out of his skin. He dashed from the living room and returned moments later with Anunciata, a large-toothed young woman with shiny blonde hair. She said: 'Oh my God, it's amazing to finally meet you!' Or rather, it was: 'Ooooooh my Goooooord, it's aaaah-maaaaazing to finally meet yaaaaaaw!' The woman's accent is unbelievably posh – her vowel sounds are so long you could take a nap in the middle of them. However, I was determined to suppress my prejudices and make our guest feel at home (or, at least, one of her homes), so I bowed deeply and led her into the dining room.

As we tucked into our meal, I tried to put Anunciata's mind at ease by telling her that, despite my job, there would be no politics talk. I said: 'You may see me as a wild-eyed revolutionary and I may wish to expropriate your parents' unearned wealth, but there's no reason we can't break bread together.'

Strangely, this didn't seem to make her any more comfortable, so I began to deploy some of my *Tatler* learning. I asked where her horses were stabled, what her dad's favourite tax haven was and whether she went to exclusive nightclubs with her mates, who I presumed were called things like Binky and Chlamydia. I even attempted to mask my earthy Shropshire accent with something a bit more RP. The Boy said: 'Dad, what's happened to your voice? Are you having a stroke?'

Once Anunciata had left, I opined to Mrs Corbyn that the night had gone well, all things considered. The Boy rounded on me, as impassioned as I've ever seen him, and said: 'Christ, Dad, why did you act so weird? How hard would it have been to treat her like a human being?'

I was rather stung by this, considering all my efforts to bridge the class divide. I said: 'In life, as in politics, I treat everyone like a human being.'

He said: 'Oh please! You spend all your time being holier-than-thou and banging on about "the people", but when it comes to actual people, you haven't got a clue!'

With that, he charged off to his room and refused to come out, even when I offered him a pack of yogurt-coated prunes from Planet Organic.

23rd December

Arrived at the office to find the atmosphere far cheerier than usual. I asked Julian why everyone seemed so chipper and he ventured that it was because 'this godawful year is nearly over'. John

McD concurred, saying: 'The last twelve months have put the "anus" in *annus horribilis*,' which I thought was good, if unnecessarily vulgar.

I'll admit that 2016 has been a year of trials and tribulations. Aside from anything else, The Boy has been staying with Anunciata for the past week and refuses to speak to me (except to request money).

After lunch, Julian came into my office and, to my great surprise, presented me with a Christmas present! I unwrapped it, only to find a Birzman Velocity mini bike pump (with its own gauge!). He looked bashful and murmured: 'No big deal, it's just, you said the other day that yours keeps, like, sticking?'

Putting aside my anti-consumerist beliefs, I felt very touched by this gesture and regretted not having bought him anything. Just then, I remembered that I had a packet of pumpkin seeds stashed in my pocket. Producing them with a flourish, I explained that Julian would now be able to start an allotment of his own. More importantly, I said, these seeds were a symbol: 'Because when you sow them and water them and carefully tend to them over weeks and months, what do you get?'

He said: 'Pumpkins.'

I said: 'Yes, pumpkins, but also something greater than that. A sense of how, like our operation here, magical things can grow from the most unexpected source.'

Julian pointed out that he would, in fact, expect pumpkins to grow from pumpkin seeds. Still, I think the lad was touched. Well done, Jeremy, on the quick thinking!

25th December, Christmas Day

Bit of a sombre Christmas this year. The Boy remains uncommunicative. Mrs Corbyn is cross because I mangled the tree while cycling home with it. Plus, I've had a tremendous dearth of cards – clearly I'm not on many MPs' lists this year. I suppose I can comfort myself with the thought that I'm doing my bit for conservation.

Still, it's important to remember that Christmas isn't just about jollity and larks. It's also a time for reflection. What have I learned from this tumultuous twelvemonth? Firstly, that 99.9 per cent of people paid to write about politics have no clue what they're talking about. Secondly, that anyone attempting to bring real socialist change to this country will be subject to constant abuse, not just from the forces of the status quo, but also those ostensibly on their side. At times, I've felt like a piñata at a birthday party where all the kids are on steroids. And what do I have to show for it? They say that whatever doesn't kill you just makes you stronger, but I find this unconvincing. Surely something that doesn't kill you can just as easily cause life-changing injuries and vast emotional trauma. It's also said that you should keep your friends close and your enemies closer. The thing is, though, I hate my enemies. Horrible bunch of people. They're all exceptionally mean to me and I'd rather not have them around.

Still, what a year it's been! The UK has thrown itself into a bottomless pit of xenophobia and political confusion. The US has cast off any pretence of being civilised by replacing erudite Obama with a perverted game-show host. The Middle East remains racked with violent instability and tensions on the Korean peninsula may well cause a world-ending nuclear conflict. On the other hand, my neglected allotment yielded a small but surprisingly delicious crop of beetroot, so it's not all doom and gloom. Here's to 2017. In the words of the band D:Ream, things can only get better ...

2017

Chapter Fifteen

The Leader's Office attempts a relaunch. I mount a charm offensive against the media, but am considered more offensive than charming. President Trump takes office.

1st January

I have decided that the new year will see a new Jeremy. My main resolution is to run a tighter ship. No more distractions or unforced errors. I will be polite and conciliatory to the Blairites (unless they mention the war in Iraq, academies or Tony Blair). I will be a model of discipline and only visit the allotment once a week (well, maybe twice every other week – no sense trying to go cold tofu). I will even do my best to accommodate journalists. They may be mendacious, venal and amoral creatures, but they're just trying to do their jobs. Their vile, deceitful jobs.

With regard to Mrs Corbyn, I am conscious that it is not always easy being married to me. I don't go to restaurants, I barely drink and I don't dance (rhythm being a bourgeois affectation). For a socialist, I must admit I can be rather unsociable! My point is, old Jez could be a lot more fun to be around. Mrs Corbyn is an excellent comrade and an even better wife and I'm lucky to have her.

Then there's The Boy. I know that it's perfectly natural for a child to grow apart from you (especially when they're in their thirties), but it does alarm me how little we have in common these days. It would seem that the charming wee mite who used to gurgle in his crib as I read him *The Condition of the Working Class in England* has been replaced with a stranger. Last Tuesday, I thought I saw him browsing the *FT* on his iPad! Still, I am first and foremost a husband and a father, so I must strive to understand my son as he is, rather than as I would like him to be. Whatever path The Boy chooses, I will always love and be proud of him. If only there were some way I could get that across. I suppose I could tell him about my feelings, but what am I, an American?

9th January

Back to the Leader's Office, full of vim and vigour. However, the first thing I spotted gave me pause. On Julian's desk there stood a plastic doll with an enormous head, a white beard and a beige suit covering its spindly limbs. Julian followed my gaze and, in a bright tone, said: 'Pretty cool, right? It's a Corbyn figurine. My mum got me one for Christmas.' With this, he picked up the thing and shook it, causing its bespectacled cranium to oscillate in an ungodly manner. Noticing my expression, Julian looked perturbed. He said: 'Don't you like it?'

No, Diary, I did not – not because it was an unflattering caricature of me, but because I don't agree with the use of plastics in the manufacturing of toys. After some discussion, we agreed that, as a compromise, Julian would keep the thing in his desk drawer.

At 3 p.m. I attended – with no great enthusiasm – a meeting to discuss my 'relaunch'. In an attempt to put everyone at ease with a bit of small talk, I asked Sally about her Christmas break. She said:

'I mainly spent it reading polling data and taking anti-anxiety meds.'

After a short pause, we moved on to business. Sally said: 'As everyone here knows, last year was a conveyor belt of disasters. It was essentially the *Hindenburg* crashing into the *Titanic*. However, that ends now. This is Corbyn 2.0. All of the inexplicable appeal to young people, none of the constant screw-ups.'

I said: 'Now, Sally, all I can be is myself.'

She said: 'Oh, believe me, I know. That's why we need to change the narrative. We tried selling you as competent. You know how that turned out. So now the idea is to position you as a Trump-style anti-establishment warrior.'

I asked, rather ironically, if she would also like me to get a spray tan and a wig. She said: 'To be honest, Jeremy, I'd like you to do anything that gets your approval rating out of minus figures.'

Pretty uncalled for.

10th January

Went on *Good Morning Britain* to tout our latest policy, a maximum wage cap. The major drawback was having to interact with Piers Morgan. Now there's someone who could do with a wage cap! His career trajectory never ceases to amaze me – literally no one likes him, yet he's always becoming richer and more famous. It's as though the bubonic plague somehow won the Nobel Peace Prize. The man acts like he was created in a lab by Osama bin Laden and Skeletor to make themselves look less hateful.

Today's other major development is the so-called Steele dossier, which claims that the Russian FSB has *kompromat* on Donald Trump. I said to my colleagues: 'Considering the things we already know about him, what on earth could be used as blackmail?'

John McD explained that the most salacious detail in the report was that Trump had participated in something called a 'golden shower'. Being unfamiliar with the term, I had to have it explained to me. I said: 'Gosh, that sounds terribly unhygienic. All *I* need to enjoy a shower is a tube of Radox and perhaps a loofah. Why on earth would Trump want such a thing?'

Julian said: 'It's mainly about the transgressive thrill that comes from being degraded.' Then, after

a beat, he continued: 'At least, according to some …
articles I read …'

To fill the ensuing silence, I said: 'I simply don't
understand how people derive sexual pleasure
from humiliation. That's just not my bag.'

Sally said: 'If it was, that would explain most of
your time as leader.'

Now, why should that get a laugh when none of
my excellent puns do?

20th January

Donald Trump was inaugurated today. Very macabre.
The rain fell in agreement with every sane person
watching. As he groped the Bible with a tiny hand,
his wife Melania stood next to him, looking frozen
as a hostage. It would hardly have been a surprise
if she'd started blinking in Morse code.

Then came the inaugural address. Trump
spoke of 'America first', of 'crime and drugs and
gangs' and border walls that need to be built.
He kept mentioning 'American Carnage', which
sounds, more than anything, like a wrestling
event. I half expected someone to sneak up and hit
him with a metal folding chair. During all of this,

the Clintons looked as though they'd swapped places with their figures from Madame Tussauds, while Obama seemed to have aged by approximately fifty years. Apparently, once Trump had concluded, George W. Bush was heard to remark: 'That was some weird shit.' I would hesitate to say that it was weirder shit than, say, setting most of the Middle East on fire, but that's a matter of opinion. Still, while Trump has yet to do anything a thousandth as bad as Bush Jr., I have no doubt that he has it in him.

One thing I kept thinking was this: if something so implausibly bad as Trump's election can happen, does that mean something implausibly good could happen too? With the world in such a state of flux, is real socialist change achievable? Or maybe we're all just going to die! That's a joke. I think ...

27th January

Today the Prime Minister travelled to the White House to meet with this awful Trump character. Theresa may be a cold-hearted, austerity-mad Tory, but I couldn't help feeling sorry for her.

Julian showed me a photo where the guy was clutching her hand, having been spooked by a ramp. I'm not sure I'd be willing to hold Trump's hand, not least because I don't want fake tan all over me.

Chapter Sixteen

Our relaunch comes crashing to earth. The Boy and I are both glum, but for separate reasons. The PM triggers the mysterious Article 50.

30th January

Had a truly appalling encounter with the mainstream media today. Sally was keen to roll out the new, improved Corbyn 2.0 so had booked me to appear on Radio 4. As ever, I was to be interviewed by some featureless BBC news droid. Any hope I might have had of receiving fair treatment disappeared as soon as he asked his first question: 'Mr Corbyn, how can you hope to lead your party to victory when it spent much of last year trying to oust you?'

I said: 'Look, the Labour Party is like a family. Families often have disagreements, but that doesn't mean they love each other any less. Sometimes a family will try and put grandpa in a nursing home, because they think he's lost his marbles. But then they realise that, actually, he knows exactly what he's doing and they say: "Sorry, Grandpa, we now see that you *should* be prime minister."' At this point, I became aware of frantic movement inside the engineer's booth. Glancing up, I saw a white-faced Sally repeatedly drawing a finger across her neck.

The interviewer continued: 'Labour is currently divided between those who fervently oppose Brexit and those who feel your party should embrace it, for fear of ceding working class votes to UKIP. What do you say to Labour supporters who wish to stay in the EU?'

I said: 'You're asking what people think about Brexit, and I'd say the key word there is "people". We have to listen to what people are saying. After all, one can't spell EU without U. As in you, the people.' Just then, I heard a series of dull thuds and looked up to see Sally banging her head against the glass partition.

The interviewer looked bemused and continued: 'Moving on, the Prime Minister has said that Brexit means Brexit, but many are unclear what Brexit means to you. If Brexit is the will of the people, do you think it should be hard or soft? Or would you favour one of the Norwegian, Swiss or Canadian models?'

I said: 'What people really care about isn't Norwegian models, it's whether this is a Brexit that will preserve the rights of British workers. I will not support any Brexit that makes working people in this country worse off.'

He said: 'What kind of Brexit would make things better for them?'

I paused, then said: 'I'd love to answer that, but I'm afraid we've run out of time, haven't we?'

He said: 'We're scheduled for five more minutes.'

Glancing at Sally, I saw that she was standing stock still, with her jaw hanging open.

I thought I was in for a telling-off on the drive back to Westminster, but Sally just sat there in silence. I said: 'Well, that was fairly rough, but what do you expect from the Biased Broadcasting Corporation?'

She let out a low moan and said: 'I'll never work in British politics again.'

31st January

Yet more drama, this time on the domestic front. I came downstairs this morning to find The Boy looking pallid and dishevelled. The lad clearly hadn't slept, so naturally I enquired what was wrong. He replied, with a forced careless air, that he and Anunciata had broken up. I said I was awfully sorry to hear that and asked what had caused it. With a roll of his eyes and a theatrical sigh, he said: 'Political differences.'

Putting a consoling hand on his shoulder, I said: 'I always suspected this would happen, but I take no pleasure in being right. The fact is that the two of you are from different worlds: you're upper-middle class and she's middle-upper class. It was never going to work.'

He didn't respond and instead regarded his muesli with a listless gaze. Seeking another tack, I said: 'At least now you'll have more time to work on your app.'

He said: 'What's the point? Without Nun's parents bankrolling it, I'm screwed. And all the City lads stopped talking to me after you announced that wage cap!'

Of course, it pains me to see my son go through heartbreak. I wish there was some way I could lighten his load. But perhaps this is a necessary hardship on the way to him meeting someone more appropriate, like a trade union rep or a beautiful South American freedom fighter.

1st February

Former ExxonMobil CEO Rex Tillerson has been confirmed as US Secretary of State. Nice of Trump to abandon even the pretence that multinational corporations aren't in charge. Of course, whenever I've said that the world is controlled by oil companies rather than democratic governments, it was dismissed as leftie nonsense ...

Trump's cabinet now contains multiple billionaires. I hope they don't bully those poor cabinet members who are merely millionaires! If it was up to me, there wouldn't be any millionaires *or* billionaires. To be honest, I'm not even sure how I feel about thousandaires.

2nd February

While flicking through these pages, I chanced upon the limerick I wrote back in June. Thinking it was rather good (apart from the last line, which went somewhat off-kilter), I decided to have another go:

LIMERICK #2
By Jeremy Corbyn

One of the left's brightest sparks
Was this German fellow, Karl Marx.
He gave it his best go
With his manifesto
Which interprets history as a perpetual class struggle
between the proletarians and the bourgeoisie.

Still not perfect, but I'm getting better! I read it to The Boy in the hope of cheering him up, but he didn't even crack a smile. Given the funniness of the poem, this is very worrying.

4th February

The Boy still exceedingly gloomy. The only time he leaves his room is to get another craft beer from the fridge. He reminds me of how I felt when the USSR collapsed! It being Saturday, I decided to take him out to the allotment. I had hoped that being among the miracles of nature would lift his spirits, as it always does mine, but no such luck. He barely had the wherewithal to tilt his watering can. After a while, I realised that a pep talk was in order. I said:

'Son, I brought you out here so we could speak man to man. Look, I know that you're hurting. I've been through a fair few breakups myself. Admittedly, most of them happened because I was marching at too many demonstrations or wouldn't stop talking about Venezuela, but I understand your pain.'

He said: 'I still can't believe it. I thought Nun was the one.'

I said: 'Well, life has a habit of throwing you curveballs. I was a backbencher for thirty-two years. I never had so much as a sniff of ministerial office. Who would have thought I'd end up being in charge of the Labour Party? I mean, a lot of people would say I'm not in charge of the Labour Party, but still ...'

At this point, The Boy burst into tears, which was very disconcerting. I wasn't sure what to do, so I patted him on the back and said: 'Solidarity.'

9th February

Big day at the office: the Commons has passed a bill to 'trigger Article 50'. Still not entirely sure what that means – it sounds exciting, like something James Bond would do, but in practice it's incredibly boring. Not wanting to defy the will of the people,

I imposed a three-line whip to make sure the party went along with it. The PLP are pretty upset about this, so I was keen to avoid getting collared after the vote.

Sneaking through the Members' Lobby, I spotted a red-faced Tom Watson. Thinking on my feet, I hid behind the statue of H. H. Asquith until the sound from Tom's Dre Beats headphones had subsided. Moving into the Central Lobby, I was spotted by Laura Kuenssberg, who shouted, 'Mr Corbyn, what is your personal position on Brexit?' and chased me down a corridor.

Knowing that I would be unable to outrun the frightening Scottish news lady, I opted to hide in a nearby cupboard. While attempting to catch my breath, I noticed that someone else was in there: 'Michael Gove? What are you doing here?'

He replied: 'Oh, I'm hiding from Boris. I duck in here every time I see him. The guy's out of shape, but if he fell on you ... Game over.'

10th March

Given how hard I've been working recently, I decided to treat myself to a snazzy new hat of the

Panama variety. Though, at £20, it far exceeds my usual clothes budget, I must say I like the effect. When I looked in the shop's mirror, I saw a suave bohemian poet gaze back at me. *¡Muy guapo, Jeremy!*

11th March

It being the weekend and the sun having made one of its rare appearances, I thought the time was right to debut my hat. I popped the thing on my head, set it to a jaunty angle and strode down to the kitchen. After a beat, The Boy started laughing uproariously and said: 'Bloody hell, Dad, you look like the man from the Dolmio ads!'

While this jibe was obviously uncalled for, Mrs Corbyn and I were glad to see him so engaged. With any luck, he'll soon be back to his old self (for better or worse).

17th March

George Osborne, that slimy boarding school sadist, has been named editor of the *Evening Standard*! Good to know that the most widely read paper in

London will now function as a sort of posh-boy *Pravda* ...

I can't say 2017 has been a massive improvement on its predecessor thus far. My days are all Brexit, Brexit, Brexit. The discussions are at once bafflingly vague and crushingly technical. Even my best friends wouldn't claim that I'm a detail-oriented guy, so I just nod along with what I'm told. After a particularly frustrating meeting, Diane said: 'How are we meant to defend your position when no one knows what it is?'

The Boy continues to languish in his room, sighing and listening to the Smiths. I can't stand Morrissey myself – the man gives humourless, preachy vegetarians a bad name!

29th March

Theresa May has signed a letter triggering Article 50 (which I've just now got to grips with). This is a highly consequential moment in our nation's history, but you wouldn't know it from the robotic monotone in which she made the announcement. Commentators are always saying I lack charisma, but this woman makes me look like Muhammad Ali ...

12th April

Like one of those Hammer horror films where Dracula fights Frankenstein's monster, today's news brought together the *Daily Mail* and Donald Trump. It seems that Dacre's lot are grovelling to Melania and paying her something in the region of two million pounds in damages for publishing an article including 'false and defamatory claims that questions the nature of her work as a professional model and republished allegations that she provides services beyond simply modelling'. I'd say she got off pretty lightly – the *Mail* has called me much worse!

Chapter Seventeen

The Prime Minister makes a surprise announcement. Differing opinions on my chances of victory. I travel the country, only to discover that crowds like me more than the media.

18th April

Arrived at the office to find everyone in a state of extreme panic. I approached John and Diane and enquired as to the cause of all this wailing and gnashing of teeth. Was it the Rapture, as predicted by evangelical Christians? Were nuclear missiles about to rain down upon our heads? No, it emerged that Theresa May has announced a general election to be held on the 8th June. All around the room, staff were staring into the middle distance or frantically updating their CVs. John muttered: 'Well, that's torn it ... The jig is well and truly up.'

I argued that this was excellent news – an opportunity to take our bold, progressive vision out to the country and establish me as a viable prime minister. After a long pause, Diane said: 'Sure, Jeremy. Sure it is.'

My colleagues are just nervous because the polls have us around twenty points behind. But who cares about that? Bookies put my chance of securing the leadership at 100 to 1. When the polls say I have any hope of winning, that's when I'll start to worry!

While making tea for some of my more shell-shocked colleagues, I overheard Sally outside the kitchen, talking on her phone. She said: 'We'll obviously be annihilated – the BBC graphics department's going to run out of blue pixels. Still, at least it'll sort out the situation with you-know-who ...'

Well, dear Diary, I don't care what the nay-sayers say (mostly 'nay', I imagine). The truth is, I feel more energised than I have in a long while. After all, what's an election but a series of rallies and demonstrations and opportunities for people to chant your name? Most importantly, no one gives a damn about details!

Mrs Corbyn, as ever, has been wonderful. The moment I got home, she said: 'You are my husband

and I believe in you. I know you'll go out there, stay true to your principles and fight with everything you've got. Plus, when the election's done, we can go on a lovely long holiday together.'

I said: 'Well, not if we're moving into Downing Street.'

She paused a moment, then said: 'Yes, that definitely *could* happen ...'

20th April

Today saw our first meeting on the subject of Labour's 2017 manifesto. I am keen to adopt a non-hierarchical approach to policy, so we are accepting pitches from everyone in the office. After outlining some of my own ideas – setting up a database of good picnic spots, the establishment of a National Allotment Service, etc. – I opened the floor. There was a long silence, then Julian suggested something called the 'Corbyn footprint'.

John McDonnell said: 'What the hell is that?'

Julian said: 'Well, it's, like, a play on "carbon footprint"?'

John said: 'Yes, but what does it mean?'

Julian said: 'Could be an environment thing?'

John said: 'Enough of this piffling crap. We need to give our supporters some red meat – sorry, Jeremy, poor choice of words.'

We spent the next few hours fruitlessly searching for promises that would appeal to our base without alienating the wider electorate. Sally said: 'We could do with something that appeals to millennials.'

After a beat, Julian said: 'Nationalise Tinder?' John responded to this vituperatively.

I said: 'Now, John, there are no wrong answers.'

He said: 'Yes there are! I've been hearing them all morning!'

In the afternoon, we discussed our wider electoral strategy. There's an idea that we should set up another semi-affiliated campaign group, run by my most hardcore supporters. Julian suggested it be called 'Jezbollah' – which I think has a ring to it – but it was immediately shouted down. His other idea was an LGBT group called 'Lezzas for Jezza', though this was deemed problematic. Still, the young man's trying, and I think that's to be encouraged.

At dinner, I told Mrs Corbyn of my intention to provide several dozen jars of gooseberry jam for the upcoming Hackney Spring Festival. She said: 'Don't you think you'll be too busy, what with the election and all? Perhaps you could just make a couple of jars.'

I replied: 'No, I want to provide fruit preserves for the many, not the few.'

She asked me to repeat what I'd just said. I said: 'Fruit preserves?'

She said: 'No, the other part.'

I said: 'For the many, not the few.' She told me the phrase was catchy and might make a good slogan. I wasn't convinced, but said I would mention it to the team.

23rd April

Michael Fallon, the aggressive Secretary of Defence, has gone on Sky News to huff and puff and accuse me of being 'staggeringly irresponsible' regarding the nation's security. I would humbly suggest that there is something fairly irresponsible about invading any Middle East country with a vowel in its name, or spending incalculable amounts on weapons that could end the world several times over. This view may be unpopular, but I believe we should aspire to killing as few people as possible. Of course, saying so has painted an enormous target on my back. That's the thing about living in a militarised society: if you admit that you would even hesitate to launch £2 billion worth of missiles into an Iraqi pre-school, you get called a lily-livered hippie.

I have no idea where these people get the idea that I'm not tough. As someone who spent five years in charge of the Holloway Crocheters' Alliance, I'm no stranger to getting my hands dirty. Those old ladies could be vicious ...

24th April

Speaking of deranged militarism, Tony Blair has said that he's tempted to make a political comeback! Of course, I would be delighted for him to stand as a Labour MP. It would be ironic if *he* had to spend a decade on the backbench with *me* as leader. Ha ha! Still, I appreciate it must be difficult for Tony to see his New Labour legacy upended by an old-school socialist. Fortunately for him, he can always distract himself by doing lucrative PR work for dictators.

Campaigning in Scotland at the moment. I'm struck by the contrast between my coverage in the national press ('Calamity Corbyn') and the massive crowds that come to see me speak. It really does feel like we're building a movement – each day I look out at a sea of faces, people of every age, race and background, all screaming: 'JEZ WE CAN!' Of course, I'm a humble sort of guy, so I take no pleasure in this adulation. Well, maybe just a bit ...

27th April

Boris has made his first real contribution to the electoral discourse, which is to call me a 'mutton-headed old mugwump'. My aides and I spent about an hour trying to work out what on earth he meant. Sad to think the Tories' great hope is this love-child of a hippo and a thesaurus.

Spoke at a rally in Leeds, where, coincidentally, The Boy happens to be staying. He's also been travelling the country of late, meeting with potential investors in his app. Though I don't necessarily approve of entrepreneurship, I'm glad to see him getting out of the house and taking some initiative. Anyway, I took him out for dinner and it was just like the old days – me chiding him for his frivolous attitude; him disrespecting my beliefs, demeanour and fashion sense. I asked if he'd seen me on Channel 4 the previous night. He replied that he doesn't watch my interviews, as he's not a fan of horror films. I'm delighted to see that my son has got his verve back, even if that verve can be attributed to capitalism. You know, maybe politics isn't everything ...

Chapter Eighteen

Local elections paint a grim picture. Yet another train-based disaster. Tensions with Sally come to a head. My darkest hour.

1st May

Had a rough time on the campaign trail today. Of course, there were the usual chants of, 'NICE ONE, JEZZA!', as well as the hordes of young people wanting selfies with me (which I don't mind, even though they always make me look rather bewildered). Unfortunately, I met with a fair amount of reticence – if not outright hostility – on the doorstep. Comments included 'Posh Trot', 'Bearded liability' and 'I wouldn't trust you to run a cake sale.' The latter remark stung, given that I have organised several cake sales, all of which were very well attended.

Most frustrating was a gentleman who said: 'Sorry, Jez – I agree with pretty much everything you say, but I can't vote for you.'

I asked why not, to which he replied: 'Because you're unelectable.'

I said: 'Surely I'm only unelectable if people like you won't vote for me.'

He said, 'Yeah, well, I don't make the rules,' then closed the door in my face. I must admit this rankled and caused me to snap at Julian when he was unable to source any almond-and-chia-seed granola clusters in the middle of Rotherham.

Though I felt drained by the end of the day, my hotel room was terribly stuffy and I found myself unable to sleep. I tried to call Mrs Corbyn, but her phone went straight to voicemail. Having given it some thought, I decided to call Diane. After all, we've been through a great deal together and she always knows how to cheer me up. The phone rang a few times before she answered and said: 'For goodness' sake, Jeremy, I was fast asleep. This better be party business.'

However, her tone soon softened when she realised I was in a bit of a tizzy. I'm afraid I rather played the sympathy card and kept her talking about Soviet civil engineering until 3 a.m.

2nd May

I feel terrible for Diane! She went on Nick Ferrari's LBC show this morning to talk about police funding and – due to her exhaustion – got her numbers muddled up. Naturally the media vultures have piled onto her, with an eagerness they would no doubt replicate for a white male politician ...

The situation is all the more painful to witness, knowing that it's my fault! I would volunteer to explain to journalists what happened, but Mrs Corbyn would be furious if she knew I'd been talking to another woman about Soviet civil engineering. Feel very rotten about the whole thing.

5th May

Yesterday's council elections were a bit of a setback, all told. Labour lost about 380 councillors, while the Tories made big gains. Of course, everyone assumes this is a prelude to us getting mauled in the general. Julian seemed especially dispirited. I told him not to read too much into these results – it's just that voters who went to UKIP because the Tories weren't racist enough are returning to the fold. Plus, I said: 'Who votes in council elections? They may as well have a minimum age limit of eighty-five.'

He said: 'Sure, but what will you do if the pattern holds for this election?'

I said: 'Look, if Labour gets wiped out, that's just evidence we weren't left wing *enough*. Don't worry, I'm going nowhere.'

He still looked quite worried.

It's important that I'm brave for my staff, but I must admit to being nervous. For all that I try to take myself out of the equation, I can't say I want to be remembered as the guy who drove the party off a cliff (apart from anything, I don't have a licence).

7th May

Heartening news from the French presidential election – the *Front National*'s Marine Le Pen was handily defeated by the centrist Emmanuel Macron. Macron may be a bloodless, austerity-loving technocrat, but at least the world has been spared another Trump-style authoritarian. It's a strange feeling when the fascist coming in second feels like something to celebrate ...

9th May

Was up until 3 a.m. again last night putting the finishing touches to our manifesto. I'm rather proud of it. In fact, I'd go so far as to say it's my second favourite manifesto, after the communist one. My colleagues made me remove my idea for free sandals on the NHS, but hey, politics is about compromise.

Later: Disaster! Was re-reading the manifesto on the train when I inadvertently nodded off. Waking up, I was so groggy that I exited my carriage and left the printout on the seat next to me. Very embarrassing, as the thing is meant to be top secret until next week. Still, I'm sure it'll be fine – someone will just have binned it.

10th May

The manifesto leaked. The papers are beside themselves with glee and everyone in the office is acting like it's doomsday. I told Julian that I needed to liaise with the Deputy Leader. He said: 'Yeah, I tried to talk to Tom, but he just stormed into his office and started playing Rage Against the Machine at full volume …'

12th May

Upsetting scenes in the office today. We've been getting hammered over the manifesto leak, of course – the Tories called it 'Jeremy Corbyn's plan to unleash chaos' and the *Mail* claims I want to 'Take Britain back to the 1970s'. Surely that's better than what they want to do, which is take Britain back to the 1870s … In any case, tensions were exceedingly high when Sally called an emergency meeting this afternoon.

She looked terribly frazzled as we filed into the meeting room, and took alternating sips from a cup of coffee and a glass of Berocca. Opening her laptop and switching on the digital projector, she said: 'As you know, this manifesto leak has hugely hindered our ability to control the news cycle. However, I stayed up all last night and have come up with a media strategy to contain some of the damage. If everyone could pay attention to this PowerPoint, I will take you through—'

At this point, something very unfortunate happened. While reaching for a digestive biscuit, I accidentally knocked over my '#1 LABOUR LEADER' mug, spilling a tidal wave of ginseng tea onto Sally's keyboard. Despite my efforts to sop up the liquid, her laptop screen turned black and refused to restart. I was about to apologise for spoiling the presentation when Sally emitted a bloodcurdling cry: 'That's it! That's absolutely bloody it! I don't know why "it" is now, rather than twenty-one months ago, but it bloody well is.'

I asked what the matter was and she replied: '*You*, Jeremy! *You* are the matter. Any time someone around here looks like they want to commit *harakiri*, chances are it's because of you.'

I responded that I would replace the laptop and suggested that she was perhaps getting overly upset about this one mistake. She said: 'It's not one mistake, though, is it? It's dozens of them, every single day. Mistake after mistake, until I can barely remember what a competent operation looks like. Because you don't care about this job, not really. You don't care about winning power or running the country. All you care about is being cheered at demos and reinforcing your own sense of moral bloody righteousness. You're not a leader – you're a student protester!'

I calmly replied that she had raised some interesting points, but this only seemed to make her angrier. She said: 'I can't go on with this charade any longer. I resign. And since I no longer work for the Leader of the Opposition, I might as well say that

I've been telling the papers how dreadful you are this whole time. As has pretty much everyone in the office. They all want rid of you, Jeremy. And – thank God – they'll get their wish come June the 8th.'

With that, she left, her laptop dripping herbal tea behind her.

I stayed in my office long after everyone else went home. Slumped in my chair, staring at my portrait of Karl Marx, it seemed inevitable that Labour would be annihilated come election day. I would then be deposed, another socialist consigned to the dustbin of history, and Britain would once again have no voice for the working class. These dark thoughts could have continued indefinitely, had I not heard a soft knock on the door. I opened it to find Julian, who I'd assumed had left hours ago.

He handed me a mug of lemongrass tea and asked if I would be needing anything else this evening. I said, 'Thank you, no,' then, as he made to leave, called out: 'Julian?'

He turned back to face me. I said: 'Look, I just wanted to thank you for your solidarity. Too often I've spoken to you in a way that doesn't befit a comrade – a valued comrade. And I'm sorry you have to read about how rubbish we are every day. To be honest, I'm not sure why you put up with me.'

He paused, then said: 'Well, I'm not going to pretend you're the easiest person to work for. Or the least infuriating. But remember: before I was your assistant, I volunteered for your campaign. I did that because I believed in your message and I believed in you as a politician. You may not be the most competent, the most articulate, the most tele-genic, the wittiest, the best dressed, the—'

I said: 'I said I got the point.'

He continued: 'But one thing I've never doubted is that you care about making the world a less awful place. That's why I supported you then and that's why I support you now.'

Feeling the prickle of tears in my eyes, I murmured, 'Thanks,' and feigned fascination with the copy of *The Ethical Birdwatcher* on my desk. A smile spread across Julian's round, rosy-cheeked face and he headed off home.

13th May

My sense of gloom was only intensified by reports that Trump has dropped a so-called MOAB ('mother of all bombs') in Syria. As ever, the mainstream media and foreign policy establishment are falling over themselves to proclaim the act 'serious-minded' and 'presidential'. Their motto is forever 'Do something', so they applaud any use of military force, even if it's just blowing up a random hill and its neighbouring villagers. I imagine the President will soon be tweeting: 'Tremendous reviews for my very excellent bombing of Syria. Everyone was very happy with it, including all those people I just vaporised.'

Incidentally, it's disgusting how gleeful the American news anchors look while repeating the phrase 'mother of all bombs'. Only in the US would they give a pet name to an instrument of mass death. What's next? My Little Warhead? Bomby McBomb-face? But maybe that's just what people want these days – a spray-tanned TV presenter doling out death as his addled brain sees fit. Maybe I'm nothing but an anachronism, a leftist fuddy-duddy harking back to some time nobody cares about.

P.S. El Gato just did a wonderfully amusing sneeze, which cheered me up no end.

Chapter Nineteen

We officially launch our manifesto. The Tories launch theirs and immediately wish they hadn't. Signs of hope as I acquire a theme song.

16th May

Today the Labour manifesto was released again – intentionally this time. As unnerving as the leak may have been, I've come to think it was really a godsend. The British media has been awash with our pledges: scrapping tuition fees, increasing taxes on the rich, renationalising the railways and providing universal free childcare. So what if most of the coverage has been negative? While Murdoch's monocle may pop out at the thought of such policies, I'd say the British public rather like them.

17th May

A weird (and rather wonderful) dream last night. As before, I was lying in bed when I became conscious of another presence in the room. I called out to the spectre: 'Clarkson! Is that you again?'

He turned to me and, in a deep, treacle-rich voice, replied: 'Far from it, dear boy!'

Instantly recognising his snow-white hair and mischievous smirk, as well as the black pipe he held in his hand, I cried out: 'Tony Benn!'

Yes, it was the left-wing firebrand, my former mentor, just as I remembered him! I asked why he was visiting me. He said: 'I wanted to tell you to keep up the good work. I wish I'd lived to see a proper socialist back in charge of the party.'

I said: 'That's very kind of you, but I'm not sure my work's been all that good. We're way behind in the polls and everyone seems to think I'm an idiot.'

He said: 'Listen, you may have the political talents of a decomposing baboon, but that's hardly the point. I was never PM, nor even Labour leader. Still, I like to think I made some small difference by putting across my beliefs as strongly as I could. You have the opportunity to make a far greater difference – just go out there, be brave of heart, and remember the convictions that brought you to this point.'

I said: 'Thanks, Tony!'

He said: 'That's quite all right. Also, sorry that son of mine has been such a dick to you.'

I said: 'Not to worry. I know how difficult sons can be. Mine's trying to build this app and I've got no idea—'

Here he cut me off, saying, 'Well, I really should be going,' and with a puff of his pipe, he disappeared into thin air.

I woke with a smile on my lips and a renewed sense of determination.

18th May

The Tories have put out their own manifesto, which is less a document than a nuclear missile fired at their own foot. We sat around the office, hooting with derision as we read one dreary, misbegotten policy after another. The most eye-catching is a plan to make the elderly pay for care with the value of their homes, which the press are already calling the 'Dementia Tax'.

John said: 'This is brilliant! The only thing they could have done to alienate pensioners more is put a tax on Werther's Originals, or ban the use of racial slurs at Christmas dinner!'

And that's not all: they're also pledging to cut free school meals. Diane said: 'Margaret Thatcher was a milk snatcher – now Theresa's coming back for the rest of it!'

On top of everything else, their manifesto promises a vote to reverse the ban on fox hunting. 'Fox hunting!' John said. 'Who do they think that's going to win over? The kind of deranged toffs who base their personality on tearing apart small mammals were always going to vote Tory.'

Julian said: 'People are going mad about it online – the memes are brutal!'

I said that I still wasn't entirely sure what a meme was, but would take all the support I could get. Diane then read out something she'd spotted on Twitter: 'If you were a Conservative who secretly wanted Jeremy Corbyn to be prime minister, this is exactly the manifesto you'd write!'

20th May

Bit of a departure for me today! I made a surprise appearance at Prenton Park, home of Tranmere Rovers football team, opening for a band called the Libertines. Initially I read their name as 'the Librarians' and was somewhat disappointed when I realised my mistake. Still, very decent of them to let me borrow the spotlight. As we were driven over, Julian expressed his concern that the crowd, being 'hyped up' to see a rock-and-roll band, might be displeased when a middle-aged politician came out on stage. He said: 'Those audiences can be super rowdy – I once got knocked out at a Belle and Sebastian gig. Aren't you worried about getting bottled?'

I said: 'I wasn't until you said that ...'

It turned out these concerns were entirely unnecessary. The assembled young people greeted me with a colossal roar and continued to cheer as I spoke to them about equality, justice and decency. After a while, I became aware of a peculiar sound: soft at first, then impossible to ignore. 'Ohhhhh, Je-rem-eeeee Corrr-byn! Ohhhhh, Je-rem-eeeee Corrr-byn!' It's a remarkable feeling to hear thousands of people singing your name, and – I must confess – not an unpleasant one. I don't think I've felt such a surge of adrenaline since I won 'Largest Marrow' at the Tufnell Park fete.

After the gig had finished, I was introduced to Pete Doherty in the green room. Very nice young man, though he seemed exhausted – all fidgety, with great big bags under his eyes. I imagine touring in a band must be almost as tiring as an election campaign! After a while, he popped to the bathroom and emerged looking a lot more energised.

21st May

Apparently this Corbyn chant is spreading like wildfire! In the office, I expressed amazement that such a catchy tune had sprung up organically. Julian said: 'Well, the tune's not original – it's "Seven Nation Army".'

I said: 'Is that some kind of NATO thing? Because I don't want people associating me with militarism.' He explained that it was a song by the American band the White Stripes and played me some of their album *Elephant* (a bit too hectic for my liking).

Tom Watson popped round in the afternoon and seemed even more off with me than usual. I asked if anything was the matter, to which he replied: 'No offence, Jeremy, but I can't believe you're getting songs dedicated to you. Why not me? I've been a fan of the Stripes since they released *De Stijl*, plus I've listened to all Jack White's solo stuff!'

22nd May

Theresa's having a tough time – the outcry at the Dementia Tax has forced her to make a U-turn, while doing her best to pretend she's going straight. I felt a twinge of sympathy as I watched coverage of the press laying into her.

'Nothing has changed!' she cried repeatedly, while karate-chopping the air for emphasis. The upshot is that the PM, having run on a platform of being strong and stable, now looks about as robust as a building whose foundations are made of wet cake.

Fun rally today. Afterwards, while I was shaking hands, a young woman lifted the sleeve of her T-shirt and showed me a tattoo of the initials J.C. I said I was very grateful she had gone to the effort. She said: 'Well, actually, I got it back in the Nineties, when I was massive Pulp fan – Jarvis Cocker, you see? But nowadays I tell everyone it stands for you.'

Back in the car, Julian and I tried to think of other famous people with my initials. I came up with Jesus Christ and Johnny Cash (neither of whom I mind being compared to), while Julian came up with Jimmy Carr and James Corden (both of whom I very much do).

26th May

Happy birthday to me! I am now sixty-eight years young. So, what have I learned over the course of my nearly seven decades on this earth? Firstly, that, under the 1908 Small Holdings and Allotments Act, where there is demand, it is the duty of the local authority to provide residents, registered on the electoral roll, with allotment space. Also, the importance of crop rotation and keeping your soil pH at around 6.5. However, the truly essential knowledge I've gained is moral, rather than agricultural. When one has an opportunity to be kind, one should always take it. One must bear in mind that every living person is fighting their own inner battle. Most importantly of all, one must stand up for those in need, even when doing so isn't convenient or politically smart. Especially then. I may not always live up to these principles, but they remain an inextricable part of me. Call me a bearded buffoon, a tedious Trot, whatever you like. In the end, you can't deny that I care.

Sixty-eight years, though! In 1949, when I was born, Britain was being tortured on the rack of austerity, anti-Russian paranoia was on the rise and the American Empire wreaked havoc across the globe. Perhaps things haven't changed all that much ...

Chapter Twenty

The last days of campaigning. Thoughts on the eve of the election. A consequential dinner with Mrs Corbyn and The Boy. Life springs yet another surprise, in the form of an exit poll. I look towards the future and come to a decision.

5th June

Theresa continues to blink and grimace her way through a series of painful interviews. During a sit-down with Julie Etchingham of ITV's *Tonight* programme, the PM was asked what the naughtiest thing she ever did as a child was. She replied that she and her friends used to run through fields of wheat. My colleagues all found this hilarious (Julian dashed off to generate some lacerating memes), but, on this occasion, I happen to agree with Mrs May. Think of the poor agricultural workers who had to deal with that mess!

John said: 'So, Jeremy, what's the naughtiest thing *you* ever did?'

I replied that I struggled to think of anything notable. He said: 'Oh come on, surely there's something. You lived in Jamaica in your early twenties – you must have smoked a bit of weed.'

As a matter of fact, I never touched the stuff. Not because I have any moral objection to the recreational use of drugs, but because I'd read that cannabis causes memory loss and, as a geography teacher, was concerned this might make me forget about sedimentary rock or oxbow lakes.

Spent much of the afternoon in my office, trying to think of my most sinful deed. Eventually, I concluded that it was August 1971, when I forgot to pay my dues to the National Union of Tailors and Garment Workers. Of course, I paid double the next month, but the sense of shame still lingers.

6th June

Recalling Julian's kindness towards me during my darkest moment on the campaign (as well as his exemplary service more generally), I decided to give him a surprise. I went over to his desk and cleared my throat, sending him scrambling to minimise the window he'd been watching Netflix on. I told him that I knew I hadn't always been easy to work for, and so wished to give him a token of my appreciation. I said: 'You remember my acquaintance Stormzy? Well, I asked if he could do me a favour.'

With that I produced my present: a signed copy of Stormzy's album *Gang Signs & Prayer*, dedicated 'To Julian'. The lad responded with a display of emotion that made me profoundly uncomfortable. Still, I'm glad he liked it.

7th June

Election night eve. I must admit I'm rather nervous. This morning, I was so preoccupied I could barely enjoy my bowl of unsalted quinoa porridge. To ease my troubled mind, as well as make up for time lost on the campaign trail, I dined this evening with Mrs Corbyn and The Boy. The former supervised me in preparing a vegetarian curry and seemed genuinely chuffed with the results. The latter seemed brighter and more full of vim than he has in a long time. Apparently his app is now fully financed and ready to go on the market. But, he said: 'That's not the main reason I'm happy ...'

With a sly grin, he revealed that he has got engaged to Anunciata Basildon-Wyck! Of course, I was flabbergasted. I said: 'But you broke up!'

He replied: 'Yep, and now we're unbroken. For the rest of our lives, I should hope!'

Was I pleased? Of course I was. Still, I can't deny that my joy was mixed with sadness. The Boy – my boy – was getting married and I would have to surrender him to a world of upper-class manners and reactionary beliefs. In a quiet voice, I said: 'Forgive me, I'm very happy for you, but ... I thought you two had political differences?'

He said: 'Oh yes, Nun's quite a bit more left wing than me. In fact, I think she could give you a run for your money!'

I could only blink with disbelief and wonder if my ears were deceiving me, so The Boy continued: 'Yeah, she's a full-on Trotskyite. Obviously we have to keep it on the down-low because of her parents, but she's been making me read Eagleton, Adorno, Althusser ... In fact, she's the one who gave me the idea for my app – it's called RedFlag and it sends the user quotes from *Das Kapital* throughout their day.'

THE EMBRACE

I didn't need to hear any more. With tears falling down my cheeks, I gave my son a bear hug and declared: 'You must marry her right away!'

8th June

Election day. Despite a long, contented sleep, I awoke with the weight of the world on me. I like to think of myself as someone blessed with more than the usual consignment of zen, but this morning I felt wary of exiting my front door, passing my unruly rosebush and presenting myself to the world outside. I had been staring into the hallway mirror for some time when Mrs Corbyn came up and put her arms around me. I said: 'Does this face look prime ministerial to you?'

She said: 'You look like a Jeremy. In fact, I'd say that you were the Jeremiest Jeremy who ever Jeremied.'

I replied: 'Would you say that's a good thing?'

She smiled and handed me my Lenin cap, then said: 'I wouldn't have it any other way.'

Though I have consented to taking more car journeys of late, there's only one way I was going to travel to work today. With my feet pressed against the pedals and the wind whooshing through my hair (via the ventilated portions of my helmet, of course), I glided through the streets of Islington, my wonderful home. As I cycled, I saw people going about their days – people of every age, race, culture and class. The people it has always been my honour to serve. I just hope I haven't let them down …

Soon after arriving at the Leader's Office, I asked Julian to gather everyone round. My entire staff was there, as were John and Diane. I stood in front of them and began to speak, my voice not unstirred by emotion. I said: 'I'm not usually one for speeches – arguably a drawback in a politician – but today I'll make an exception. No one knows how this election will go. If the past couple of years have taught us anything, it's that prediction will predictably make a dick of you. But what I do know is that each and every person in this room has served their party with passion, skill and devotion. I know it's been difficult – you've put up with a lot of nonsense, most of which came from me. But even on those occasions I failed as a leader, you persevered, because you want to make this country a finer, fairer, kinder place. I appreciate that more than I can say. If you'll forgive me for using an unfashionable word, I consider every one of you a comrade. As such, I have made you each a personal pot of jam, whose flavour will, I hope, demonstrate what you mean to me.'

The staff responded with warm applause, as I knew they would. I may not be the world's leading orator, but I have always believed in the power of jam. John clapped me on the shoulder and Diane said: 'Where were these people skills during the campaign?'

Day turned to night in a flurry of activity. I'm writing this at Labour HQ, as we wait for the exit poll to arrive. Our hope is that the result is less disastrous than has been projected, so we can live to fight another day. Fingers crossed. However it turns out, I'm glad to have run a principled campaign.

Later: Dear Diary, I am in a state of blissful shock. In fact, it's as much as I can do to stop my pen-hand from shaking. Soon after I finished the first part of this entry, I heard a collective intake of breath. Fearing an unprecedented rout, I rushed over to my staff, who were all gawping at their phones. John said: 'Un-bloody-believable. They're projecting a hung parliament! According to this, we'll actually take seats from the Tories!'

THE SURPRISE

There followed a stunned silence. After a while, I remarked: 'Well, we seem to have won a magnificent defeat!'

This provoked hearty gales of laughter from the room. Finally, one of my jokes gets the reception it deserves! I can't claim all the credit, though – most of us were pretty hysterical anyway. Diane gave me a hug and said: 'My God, you might actually end up being prime minister! Sorry, I shouldn't say "actually" ...'

9th June

A truly remarkable day. With the final results in, the Conservatives are down thirteen seats and we've gained thirty. The talking heads who were gleefully predicting my ruin a couple of weeks ago are now gibbering wrecks, desperately trying to fill airtime. Throughout the day, MPs who called me a loon and a loser to my face have been going on Sky News to praise me for exceeding everyone's expectations. But this isn't the time for crowing or gloating (well, maybe just a bit – screw you, Blairites!). The fact is that I have more important things to consider. It may sound ridiculous, but, throughout the entire period of my leadership, I don't think I ever truly imagined myself in Downing Street. This has now changed.

Reflecting on the events of yesterday, and the preceding weeks, I have come to an important decision. It's clear that, more than any leftist in decades, I have a real chance to reshape the UK along egalitarian lines. Whatever people may say, this isn't something I take lightly. I need to maintain an obsessive focus on my duties as leader (as well as my allotment – let's not go crazy). Which, I'm afraid, doesn't leave me time to keep recording these reminiscences. Dear Diary, you have been witness to my triumphs, my failures and my very occasional embarrassments, but this, alas, must be your final entry.

I can't think of a more appropriate way to end than with one last crack at a limerick. Here goes ...

LIMERICK #3
By Jeremy Corbyn

There once was a comrade named Corbyn
Who found his allotment absorbin',
But, when push came to shove,

He loved nothing above
The cause of equality and the promotion of human
*   rights both at home and abroad.*

Still having trouble with that last line … Hey ho, I think it sums me up well enough. Anyway, it's getting towards nine, so I'd better head to bed.

A FINAL ENTRY